1993

THE SELECTED POETRY OF YEHUDA AMICHAI

Also by Yehuda Amichai

THE
SELECTED POETRY OF
YEHUDA AMICHAI

Edited and newly translated
by Chana Bloch and Stephen Mitchell

HarperPerennial
A Division of HarperCollinsPublishers

The poems in this collection were originally published in Hebrew.

Some of these translations have been published in the following magazines: *The Atlantic, The Berkeley Monthly, Field, Ironwood, Midstream, Mississippi Review, The Nation, New Letters, The New Republic, The Paris Review, Partisan Review, Present Tense, Quarry West, Shenandoah, Threepenny Review, Tikkun,* and *Zyzzyva.* "God Has Pity on Kindergarten Children," "Of Three or Four in a Room," and "Not Like a Cypress" first appeared, in somewhat different form, in *Voices Within the Ark,* edited by Howard Schwartz and Anthony Rudolf (Avon, 1980).

Grateful acknowledgment is made to the Ingram Merrill Foundation and to the National Foundation for Jewish Culture for their financial assistance.

A hardcover edition of this book was published in 1986 by Harper & Row, Publishers.

HarperCollins books may be purchased for educational, business, or sales promotional use. For information, please call or write: Special Markets Department, HarperCollins Publishers, Inc., 10 East 53rd Street, New York, NY 10022. Telephone: (212) 207-7528; Fax: (212) 207-7222.

First HarperPerennial edition published 1992.

Designer: Sidney Feinberg

Library of Congress Cataloging-in-Publication Data
Amichai, Yehuda.
    The selected poetry of Yehuda Amichai.
    "The poems in this collection were originally
published in Hebrew"—T.p. verso.
    Includes index.
    I. Bloch, Chana.   II. Mitchell, Stephen.
III. Title.
PJ5054.A65A264   1986   892.4'16   85-45611
ISBN 0-06-096062-0 (pbk.)

92 93 94 95 96 HC 10 9 8 7 6 5 4 3 2 1

Contents

148,383

Poems, 1948–1962

Now in the Storm, Poems 1963–1968

PART TWO
edited and translated by Chana Bloch

Not for the Sake of Remembering (1971)

Behind All This a Great Happiness Is Hiding (1976)

Time (1978)

A Great Tranquillity: Questions and Answers (1980)

The Hour of Grace (1983)

From Man Thou Art and Unto Man Shalt Thou Return (1985)

Foreword

A friend of mine tells a story about some Israeli students who were called up in the 1973 Yom Kippur War. As soon as they were notified, they went back to their rooms at the University, and each packed his gear, a rifle, and a book of Yehuda Amichai's poems. It is a little hard to envision this scene: these days we don't think of soldiers as resorting to poetry under fire, and Amichai's poetry is not standard government issue. It isn't patriotic in the ordinary sense of the word, it doesn't cry death to the enemy, and it offers no simple consolation for killing and dying.

Still, I know what these young soldiers were after, because I have often found myself turning to Amichai's poetry as a kind of restorative. Pungent, ironic, tender, playful and despairing by turns, it draws me by the energy of its language, the exuberant inventiveness and startling leaps that freshen the world, making it seem a place where anything is possible. And by the humor, too—a briny Jewish humor that can set the teeth on edge. And I am attracted by a certain astringent quality of mind, a skeptical intelligence that is impatient with camouflage and pathos and self-deceit, that insists on questioning even what it loves.

Love is at the center of Amichai's world, but he is quick to grant that his mistress's eyes are nothing like the sun, that sex is at once an enticing scent and a sticky business. And Jerusalem, the beloved city, he contemplates with a mixture of love and exasperation. No one has written more intimately about this landscape—the dust and stones and the ghosts of barbed-wire fences; the Old City with its Wailing Wall and mosques and churches, its Solomon and Herod and Suleiman the Magnificent, all under a cloud of prophecy; the foreign consulates and the housing projects; the zealous black-coated Hasidim and the tourists; the brooding presence of the dead.

Amichai's way of seeing this place—and most things he writes about—from both the inside and the outside, balancing tenderness against irony, reflects his experience of two very different worlds. Born in Würzburg, Germany, in 1924, he grew up in an Orthodox Jewish home with its strict religious observance and its protective God, as inescapable as family. His father was a shopkeeper, his grandfather a farmer, and his memories of childhood (the political situation notwithstanding) idyllic. In 1936 he came to Palestine with his parents, and his adult life has been lived in the midst of the convulsive struggle of Israel to become a state, and then survive and define itself. Amichai made his living as a teacher while studying war—with the British army in World War II, with the Palmakh in the Israeli War of Independence in 1948, and with the Israeli army in 1956 and 1973. He was formed, as he would say, half by the ethics of his father and half by the cruelties of war.

Amichai's first collection of poetry appeared in 1955. Since then he has published ten volumes of poetry, as well as novels, short stories, and plays. His poems enjoy an enormous popularity in Israel. In a nation where only three million people read Hebrew, it is remarkable that each of his books sells about 15,000 copies. The poems are recited on public occasions, taught in the schools, set to music. And for a poet so rooted in his own place, his work is remarkably well known outside of Israel, having been translated into some twenty languages.

Throughout his career, he has written about memory and the burdens of memory; about the lingering sweetness and simplicity of his parents' lives set against the perplexities of his own; about war as loss and love as a hedge against loss. The most troubling loss is that of his childhood, left behind in the normal course of life and then destroyed by war. "My childhood of blessèd memory," he calls it, borrowing an expression commonly used when speaking of the dead.

Amichai holds on tightly to whatever he has lost. "What I will never see again I must love forever" is his first article of faith. That is why there are so many elegies of love. And that is why the God in these poems, who at times seems no more than a figure of speech, deeply embedded in the language, makes his presence strongly felt even in his absence. Amichai's sardonic quarrel with God is what stamps this poetry as so unmistakably Jewish. That quarrel carries on the venerable tradition of Abraham, Jeremiah, and Job.

The poems in this volume, chosen from Amichai's best work over a productive career of more than thirty years, should give some notion of his stylistic range: long poems and short, rhymed and unrhymed, in formal meters and in free verse; poem cycles; prose poems and poems hovering at the borders of prose; poems of an overflowing abundance and poems of a tightly coiled concision. All the translations are our own: Stephen Mitchell translated the poems written before 1969, and I translated the later ones. Many of these have not previously appeared in English.

Reading Amichai's poems in Hebrew, one is struck by the frequent allusions to biblical and liturgical texts. The Israeli reader, even one who has not had Amichai's formal religious education, will have studied the Bible from grade school through college, and is also likely to recognize the kind of liturgical texts that Amichai refers to, such as the Mourner's Kaddish or the Yom Kippur service. Because this is obviously not true of most readers of English, we have often borrowed from or imitated the King James Bible as a way of pointing up allusions that might otherwise have gone unnoticed. On the other hand, modern Hebrew, revived as a spoken language only a hundred years ago, is much closer to the

Hebrew of the Old Testament than our own language is to seventeenth-century English, and Amichai's allusions never have a "literary" air. So when we felt that the archaisms of the King James Version intruded awkwardly on the naturalness and ease of Amichai's diction, we have found other equivalents. And when an allusion would have required too much explanation, we have sometimes chosen to disregard it.

To write poetry in Hebrew is to be confronted with the meaning of Jewish experience in all its strangeness and complexity. Amichai's provocative allusions —ranging from the witty and mischievous ("The man under his fig tree telephoned the man under his vine") to the subversive and iconoclastic ("The army jet makes peace in the heavens")—are one way of wrestling with the angel. The necessity is imposed by the language itself; it is Amichai's achievement to have found in that wrestling his distinctive identity as a poet:

> to speak now in this weary language,
> a language that was torn from its sleep in the Bible: dazzled,
> it wobbles from mouth to mouth. In a language that once described
> miracles and God, to say car, bomb, God.

CHANA BLOCH

THE SELECTED POETRY OF YEHUDA AMICHAI

God Has Pity on Kindergarten Children

God has pity on kindergarten children.
He has less pity on school children.
And on grownups he has no pity at all,
he leaves them alone,
and sometimes they must crawl on all fours
in the burning sand
to reach the first-aid station
covered with blood.

But perhaps he will watch over true lovers
and have mercy on them and shelter them
like a tree over the old man
sleeping on a public bench.

Perhaps we too will give them
the last rare coins of compassion
that Mother handed down to us,
so that their happiness will protect us
now and in other days.

The U.N. Headquarters in the High Commissioner's House in Jerusalem

The mediators, the peacemakers, the compromise-shapers, the comforters
live in the white house
and get their nourishment from far away,
through winding pipes, through dark veins, like a fetus.

And their secretaries are lipsticked and laughing,
and their sturdy chauffeurs wait below, like horses in a stable,
and the trees that shade them have their roots in no-man's-land
and the illusions are children who went out to find cyclamen in the field
and do not come back.
And the thoughts pass overhead, restless, like reconnaissance planes,
and take photos and return and develop them
in dark sad rooms.

1

And I know they have very heavy chandeliers
and the boy-I-was sits on them and swings
out and back, out and back, out till there's no coming back.

And later on, night will arrive to draw
rusty and bent conclusions from our old lives,
and over all the houses a melody will gather the scattered words
like a hand gathering crumbs upon a table
after the meal, while the talk continues
and the children are already asleep.

And hopes come to me like bold seafarers,
like the discoverers of continents coming to an island,
and stay for a day or two
and rest . . .
And then they set sail.

Autobiography, 1952

My father built over me a worry big as a shipyard
and I left it once, before I was finished,
and he remained there with his big, empty worry.
And my mother was like a tree on the shore
between her arms that stretched out toward me.

And in '31 my hands were joyous and small
and in '41 they learned to use a gun
and when I first fell in love
my thoughts were like a bunch of colored balloons
and the girl's white hand held them all
by a thin string—then let them fly away.

And in '51 the motion of my life
was like the motion of many slaves chained to a ship,
and my father's face like the headlight on the front of a train
growing smaller and smaller in the distance,
and my mother closed all the many clouds inside her brown closet,
and as I walked up my street
the twentieth century was the blood in my veins,

blood that wanted to get out in many wars
and through many openings,
that's why it knocks against my head from the inside
and reaches my heart in angry waves.

But now, in the spring of '52, I see
that more birds have returned than left last winter.
And I walk back down the hill to my house.
And in my room: the woman, whose body is heavy
and filled with time.

The Smell of Gasoline Ascends in My Nose

The smell of gasoline ascends in my nose.
Love, I'll protect you and hold you close
like an *etrog* in soft wool, so carefully—
my dead father used to do it that way.

Look, the olive-tree no longer grieves—
it knows there are seasons and a man must leave,
stand by my side and dry your face now
and smile as if in a family photo.

I've packed my wrinkled shirts and my trouble.
I will never forget you, girl of my final
window in front of the deserts that are
empty of windows, filled with war.

You used to laugh but now you keep quiet,
the beloved country never cries out,
the wind will rustle in the dry leaves soon—
when will I sleep beside you again?

In the earth there are raw materials that, unlike us,
have not been taken out of the darkness,
the army jet makes peace in the heavens
upon us and upon all lovers in autumn.

3

Six Poems for Tamar

1

The rain is speaking quietly,
you can sleep now.

Near my bed, the rustle of newspaper wings.
There are no other angels.

I'll wake up early and bribe the coming day
to be kind to us.

2

You had a laughter of grapes:
many round green laughs.

Your body is full of lizards.
All of them love the sun.

Flowers grew in the field, grass grew on my cheeks,
everything was possible.

3

You're always lying on
my eyes.

Every day of our life together
Ecclesiastes cancels a line of his book.

We are the saving evidence in the terrible trial.
We'll acquit them all!

4

Like the taste of blood in the mouth,
spring was upon us—suddenly.

The world is awake tonight.
It is lying on its back, with its eyes open.

The crescent moon fits the line of your cheek,
your breast fits the line of my cheek.

5
Your heart plays blood-catch
inside your veins.

Your eyes are still warm, like beds
time has slept in.

Your thighs are two sweet yesterdays,
I'm coming to you.

All hundred and fifty psalms
roar halleluyah.

6
My eyes want to flow into each other
like two neighboring lakes.

To tell each other
everything they've seen.

My blood has many relatives.
They never visit.

But when they die,
my blood will inherit.

Yehuda Ha-Levi

The soft hairs on the back of his neck
are the roots of his eyes.

His curly hair is
the sequel to his dreams.

His forehead: a sail; his arms: oars
to carry the soul inside his body to Jerusalem.

But in the white fist of his brain
he holds the black seeds of his happy childhood.

When he reaches the belovèd, bone-dry land—
he will sow.

Ibn Gabirol

Sometimes pus,
sometimes poetry—

always something is excreted,
always pain.

My father was a tree in a grove of fathers,
covered with green moss.

Oh widows of the flesh, orphans of the blood,
I've got to escape.

Eyes sharp as can-openers
pried open heavy secrets.

But through the wound in my chest
God peers into the universe.

I am the door
to his apartment.

When I Was a Child

When I was a child
grasses and masts stood at the seashore,
and as I lay there
I thought they were all the same
because all of them rose into the sky above me.

Only my mother's words went with me
like a sandwich wrapped in rustling waxpaper,
and I didn't know when my father would come back
because there was another forest beyond the clearing.

Everything stretched out a hand,
a bull gored the sun with its horns,
and in the nights the light of the streets caressed
my cheeks along with the walls,
and the moon, like a large pitcher, leaned over
and watered my thirsty sleep.

Look: Thoughts and Dreams

Look: thoughts and dreams are weaving over us
their warp and woof, their wide camouflage-net,
and the reconnaissance planes and God
will never know
what we really want
and where we are going.

Only the voice that rises at the end of a question
still rises above the world and hangs there,
even if it was made by
mortar shells, like a ripped flag,
like a mutilated cloud.

Look, we too are going
in the reverse-flower-way:
to begin with a calyx exulting toward the light,
to descend with the stem growing more and more solemn,
to arrive at the closed earth and to wait there for a while,
and to end as a root, in the darkness, in the deep womb.

From We Loved Here

1
My father spent four years inside their war,
and did not hate his enemies, or love.
And yet I know that somehow, even there,
he was already forming me, out of

his calms, so few and scattered, which he gleaned
among the bombs exploding and the smoke,
and put them in his knapsack, in between
the remnants of his mother's hardening cake.

And in his eyes he took the nameless dead,
he stored them, so that someday I might know
and love them in his glance—so that I would

not die in horror, as they all had done. . . .
He filled his eyes with them, and yet in vain:
to all my wars, unwilling, I must go.

3
The lips of dead men whisper where they lie
deep down, their innocent voices hushed in earth,
and now the trees and flowers grow terribly
exaggerated, as they blossom forth.

Bandages are again torn off in haste,
the earth does not want healing, it wants pain.
And spring is not serenity, not rest,
ever, and spring is enemy terrain.

With the other lovers, we were sent to learn
about the strange land where the rainbow ends,
to see if it was possible to advance.

And we already knew: the dead return,
and we already knew: the fiercest wind
comes forth now from inside a young girl's hand.

6

In the long nights our room was closed off and
sealed, like a grave inside a pyramid.
Above us: foreign silence, heaped like sand
for aeons at the entrance to our bed.

And when our bodies lie stretched out in sleep,
upon the walls, again, is sketched the last
appointment that our patient souls must keep.
Do you see them now? A narrow boat drifts past;

two figures stand inside it; others row.
And stars peer out, the stars of different lives;
are carried by the Nile of time, below.

And like two mummies, we have been wrapped tight
in love. And after centuries, dawn arrives;
a cheerful archaeologist—with the light.

18

A preface first: the two of them, the brittle
calm, necessity, and sun, and shade,
an anxious father, cities braced for battle,
and from afar, unrecognizable dead.

The story's climax now—the war. First leave,
and smoke instead of streets, and he and she
together, and a mother from her grave
comforting: It'll be all right, don't worry.

And the last laugh is this: the way she put
his army cap on, walking to the mirror.
And was so lovely, and the cap just fit.

And then, behind the houses, in the yard,
a separation like cold-blooded murder,
and night arriving, like an afterword.

God's Hand in the World

1
God's hand is in the world
like my mother's hand in the guts of the slaughtered chicken
on Sabbath eve.
What does God see through the window
while his hands reach into the world?
What does my mother see?

2
My pain is already a grandfather:
it has begotten two generations
of pains that look like it.
My hopes have erected white housing projects
far away from the crowds inside me.
My girlfriend forgot her love on the sidewalk
like a bicycle. All night outside, in the dew.

Children mark the eras of my life
and the eras of Jerusalem
with moon chalk on the street.
God's hand in the world.

Sort of an Apocalypse

The man under his fig tree telephoned the man under his vine:
"Tonight they definitely might come. Assign
positions, armor-plate the leaves, secure the tree,
tell the dead to report home immediately."

The white lamb leaned over, said to the wolf:
"Humans are bleating and my heart aches with grief.
I'm afraid they'll get to gunpoint, to bayonets in the dust.
At our next meeting this matter will be discussed."

All the nations (united) will flow to Jerusalem
to see if the Torah has gone out. And then,

inasmuch as it's spring, they'll come down
and pick flowers from all around.

And they'll beat swords into plowshares and plowshares into swords,
and so on and so on, and back and forth.

Perhaps from being beaten thinner and thinner,
the iron of hatred will vanish, forever.

And That Is Your Glory

(Phrase from the liturgy of the Days of Awe)

I've yoked together my large silence and my small outcry
like an ox and an ass. I've been through low and through high.
I've been in Jerusalem, in Rome. And perhaps in Mecca anon.
But now God is hiding, and man cries Where have you gone.
And that is your glory.

Underneath the world, God lies stretched on his back,
always repairing, always things get out of whack.
I wanted to see him all, but I see no more
than the soles of his shoes and I'm sadder than I was before.
And that is his glory.

Even the trees went out once to choose a king.
A thousand times I've given my life one more fling.
At the end of the street somebody stands and picks:
this one and this one and this one and this one and this.
And that is your glory.

Perhaps like an ancient statue that has no arms
our life, without deeds and heroes, has greater charms.
Ungird my T-shirt, love; this was my final bout.
I fought all the knights, until the electricity gave out.
And that is my glory.

Rest your mind, it ran with me all the way,
it's exhausted now and needs to knock off for the day.

I see you standing by the wide-open fridge door, revealed
from head to toe in a light from another world.
And that is my glory
and that is his glory
and that is your glory.

Of Three or Four in a Room

Of three or four in a room
there is always one who stands beside the window.
He must see the evil among thorns
and the fires on the hill.
And how people who went out of their houses whole
are given back in the evening like small change.

Of three or four in a room
there is always one who stands beside the window,
his dark hair above his thoughts.
Behind him, words.
And in front of him, voices wandering without a knapsack,
hearts without provisions, prophecies without water,
large stones that have been returned
and stay sealed, like letters that have no
address and no one to receive them.

Not Like a Cypress

Not like a cypress,
not all at once, not all of me,
but like the grass, in thousands of cautious green exits,
to be hiding like many children
while one of them seeks.

And not like the single man,
like Saul, whom the multitude found
and made king.

But like the rain in many places
from many clouds, to be absorbed, to be drunk
by many mouths, to be breathed in
like the air all year long
and scattered like blossoming in springtime.

Not the sharp ring that wakes up
the doctor on call,
but with tapping, on many small windows
at side entrances, with many heartbeats.

And afterward the quiet exit, like smoke
without shofar-blasts, a statesman resigning,
children tired from play,
a stone as it almost stops rolling
down the steep hill, in the place
where the plain of great renunciation begins,
from which, like prayers that are answered,
dust rises in many myriads of grains.

Through Two Points Only One Straight Line Can Pass

(Theorem in geometry)

A planet once got married to a star,
and inside, voices talked of future war.
I only know what I was told in class:
through two points only one straight line can pass.

A stray dog chased us down an empty street.
I threw a stone; the dog would not retreat.
The king of Babel stooped to eating grass.
Through two points only one straight line can pass.

Your small sob is enough for many pains,
as locomotive-power can pull long trains.
When will we step inside the looking-glass?
Through two points only one straight line can pass.

13

At times *I* stands apart, at times it rhymes
with *you*, at times *we*'s singular, at times
plural, at times I don't know what. Alas,
through two points only one straight line can pass.

Our life of joy turns to a life of tears,
our life eternal to a life of years.
Our life of gold became a life of brass.
Through two points only one straight line can pass.

Half the People in the World

Half the people in the world
love the other half,
half the people
hate the other half.
Must I because of this half and that half
go wandering and changing ceaselessly
like rain in its cycle,
must I sleep among rocks,
and grow rugged like the trunks of olive trees,
and hear the moon barking at me,
and camouflage my love with worries,
and sprout like frightened grass between the railroad tracks,
and live underground like a mole,
and remain with roots and not with branches,
and not feel my cheek against the cheek of angels,
and love in the first cave,
and marry my wife beneath a canopy
of beams that support the earth,
and act out my death, always
till the last breath and the last
words and without ever understanding,
and put flagpoles on top of my house
and a bomb shelter underneath. And go out on roads
made only for returning and go through
all the appalling stations—
cat, stick, fire, water, butcher,
between the kid and the angel of death?

Half the people love,
half the people hate.
And where is my place between such well-matched halves,
and through what crack will I see
the white housing projects of my dreams
and the barefoot runners on the sands
or, at least, the waving
of a girl's kerchief, beside the mound?

For My Birthday

Thirty-two times I went out into my life,
each time causing less pain to my mother,
less to other people,
more to myself.

Thirty-two times I have put on the world
and still it doesn't fit me.
It weighs me down,
unlike the coat that now takes the shape of my body
and is comfortable
and will gradually wear out.

Thirty-two times I went over the account
without finding the mistake,
began the story
but wasn't allowed to finish it.

Thirty-two years I've been carrying along with me
my father's traits
and most of them I've dropped along the way,
so I could ease the burden.
And weeds grow in my mouth. And I wonder,
and the beam in my eyes, which I won't be able to remove,
has started to blossom with the trees in springtime.
And my good deeds grow smaller

and smaller. But
the interpretations around them have grown huge, as in

15

an obscure passage of the Talmud
where the text takes up less and less of the page
and Rashi and the other commentators
close in on it from every side.

And now, after thirty-two times,
I am still a parable
with no chance to become its meaning.
And I stand without camouflage before the enemy's eyes,
with outdated maps in my hand,
in the resistance that is gathering strength and between towers,
and alone, without recommendations
in the vast desert.

Two Photographs

1. *Uncle David*

When Uncle David fell in the First World War,
the high Carpathians buried him in snow.
And just as buried: his hard questions. So
I never found out what the answers were.

But somehow the brass buttons on his coat
opened for me. My life began far from
the pure white of his death, and like a gate

his face swung open, and because of him
I live my answer, as a part of all
that did survive, after the deep snow fell.

And he, still posing sadly as before,
dressed in the antique uniform and the
sharp helmet, seems like an ambassador
from some strange land a hundred years away.

2. *Passport Photograph of a Young Woman*

Pinned to the paper like a butterfly.
How is it your identity's still breathing

between the pages? Your mouth was set to cry
till you found out that tears spoil everything.

And held yourself, unmoved, like a death mask
or a watch no one had bothered to repair
for a long time. Did you go on living, past
that moment? For not a single person here

knows you. Well, perhaps a prince will call,
will arrive on his white horse to whisk you off,
soaring high up, above the white canal

that stretches out between your photograph
and signed name; or the embossed official stamp
will bridge that gap and be your exit-ramp.

Poems for a Woman

1
Your body is white like sand
that children have never played in.

Your eyes are sad and beautiful
like the pictures of flowers in a textbook.

Your hair hangs down
like the smoke from Cain's altar:

I have to kill my brother.
My brother has to kill me.

2
All the miracles in the Bible and all the legends
happened between us when we were together.

On God's quiet slope
we were able to rest awhile.

The womb's wind blew for us everywhere.
We always had time.

3
My life is sad like the wandering
of wanderers.

My hopes are widows,
my chances won't get married, ever.

Our loves wear the uniforms of orphans
in an orphanage.

The rubber balls come back to their hands
from the wall.

The sun doesn't come back.
Both of us are an illusion.

4
All night your empty shoes
screamed alongside your bed.

Your right hand hangs down from your dream.
Your hair is studying night-ese
from a torn textbook of wind.

The moving curtains:
ambassadors of foreign superpowers.

5
If you open your coat,
I have to double my love.

If you wear the round white hat,
I have to exaggerate my blood.

In the place where you love,
all the furniture has to be cleared out from the room,

all the trees, all the mountains, all the oceans.
The world is too narrow.

6
The moon, fastened with a chain,
keeps quiet outside.

The moon, caught in the olive branches,
can't break free.

The moon of round hopes
is rolling among clouds.

7
When you smile,
serious ideas get exhausted.

At night the mountains keep quiet beside you,
in the morning the sand goes with you down to the beach.

When you do nice things to me
all the heavy industries shut down.

8
The mountains have valleys
and I have thoughts.

They stretch out
until fog and until no roads.

Behind the port city
masts stood.
Behind me God begins
with ropes and ladders,
with crates and cranes,
with forever and evers.

Spring found us;
all the mountains around
are stone weights
to weigh how much we love.

The sharp grass sobbed
into our dark hiding-place;
spring found us.

Children's Procession

Upon the banners fluttering overhead
are verses with a day-off from all the trouble
they live with in their black and heavy Bible;
and already, in the air, the poems fade

like smoke above them, to the starting-point
where the children left behind: the trampled grass,
candy wrappers, footprints, cards, a bus,
and also a little girl in tears, who couldn't

find what she'd lost. But in the interim,
far from here, everything stopped, and then
they had to march in place, a long long time,

while at the bright edges of the birds of day
a row of angels dangled upside-down
like shirts on a clothesline; they arrived that way.

Ballad of the Washed Hair

The stones on the mountain are always
awake and white.

In the dark town, angels on duty
are changing shifts.

A girl who has washed her hair
asks the hard world, as if it were Samson,
where is it weak, what is its secret.

A girl who has washed her hair
puts new clouds on her head.

The scent of her drying hair is
prophesying in the streets and among stars.

The nervous air between the night trees
starts to relax.

The thick telephone book of world history
closes.

Sonnet from the Voyage

To V.S., captain of the Rimmon

Gulls escorted us. From time to time
one would fly down upon the waves and settle
there, like the rubber ducks when I was little
inside the bathtub of a far-off dream.

Then fog descended, all the winds were stilled,
a buoy danced and its slow ringing raised
memories of another life, effaced.
And then we knew: that we were in the world.

And the world sensed us there, with empathy;
God called to you and called to me again
with the same call, by this time almost banal,

that once addressed the patriarchs in the Bible.
We didn't answer. Even the mild rain
splashed down, as if being wasted, on the sea.

The Visit of the Queen of Sheba

1. *Preparations for the Journey*

Not resting but
moving her lovely butt,
the Queen of Sheba,
having decided to leave, a-

rose from her lair
among dark spells, tossed her hair,
clapped her hands,
the servants fainted, and
already she drew in the sand
with her big toe:
King Solomon, as though
he were a rubber ball, an
apocalyptic, bearded herring, an
imperial walking-stick, an
amalgam, half chicken
and half Solomon.

The minister of protocol
went too far, with all
those peacocks and ivory boxes.
Later on,
she began to yawn
deliciously, she stretched like a cat
so that
he would be able to sniff
her odif-
erous heart. They spared no expense,
they brought feathers, to tickle
his ears, to make his last defense
prickle.
She had been brought
a vague report
about circumcision,
she wanted to know everything, with absolute precision,
her curiosity
blossomed like leprosy,
the disheveled sisters of her corpuscles
screamed through their loudspeaker into all her muscles,
the sky undid
its buttons, she made herself up and slid
into a vast commotion,
felt her head
spin, all the brothels of her emotions
were lit up in red.
In the factory
of her blood, they worked frantically

till night came: a dark night, like an old table,
a night as eternal
as a jungle.

2. *The Ship Waits*

A ship in the harbor. Night.
Among the shadows, a white

ship, with a cargo of yearnings,
some temperate, some burning,

a ship that desire launches,
a ship without a subconscious.

Already among the sails
sway the Queen's colored veils,

made of the silk of sparrows
who had died of their tiny sorrows

before they could flutter forth
to the cool lands of the North.

It's worthwhile, at any rate,
for the white ship to wait

cheek to cheek with the dock
and let itself gently rock

between ideas of sand
and ideas of ocean, and

endure its insomnia
till morning, etc.

3. *Setting Sail*

She called her thighs to return to each other,
knee-cheek to knee-cheek, and her soul
was already a zebra of moods, good and bad.
In the oven of her body, her heart
rotated on a spit. The morning screamed,
a tropical rain fell.

23

The forecasters, chained to the spot, forecasted,
the engineers of her sleep went out on weary camels,
all the little fish of her laughter fled
before the shark of her awakening rage. In her armpits
faint-hearted corals hid,
night-lizards left their footprints on her belly.

She sat in bed, sharpening her charms and her riddles
like colored pencils. From the beards
of old blowhards, she had had an African apron made,
her secrets were embroidered on scarves.

But the lions still held the laws
like the two tablets over the holy ark
and over the whole world.

4. *The Journey on the Red Sea*

Fish blew through the sea and through
the long anticipation. Captains
plotted their course by the map
of her longing. Her nipples preceded her like scouts,
her hairs whispered to one another
like conspirators. In the dark corners between sea and ship
the counting started, quietly.
A solitary bird sang
in the permanent trill of her blood. Rules fell
from biology textbooks, clouds were torn like contracts,
at noon she dreamt about
making love naked in the snow, egg yolks dripping
down her leg, the thrill of yellow beeswax. All the air
rushed to be breathed inside her. The sailors cried out
in the foreign language of fish.

But underneath the world, underneath the sea,
there were cantillations as if on the Sabbath:
everything sang each other.

5. *Solomon Waits*

Never any rain,
never any rain,
always clouds without closure,
always raw-voiced love.

Shepherds of the wind returned
from the pasture.
In the world's court-
yards, blossoms of stone opened
consecrated to strange gods.
Trembling ladders dreamt about
humans dreaming about them.

But he
saw the world,
the slightly torn
lining of the world.
And was awake like many lit stables
in Megiddo.

Never any rain,
never any rain,
always raw-voiced love,
always quarries.

6. *The Queen Enters the Throne Room*

The dewy rose of her dark pudenda
was doubled in the mirrored floor. His agenda

seemed superfluous now, and all the provisions
he had made for her, the decrees and decisions

he had worked out while he was judging the last
of the litigants. Then he rolled up his past

like a map; and he sat there, reeling, giddy,
and saw in the mirror a body and a body,

from above and below, like the queen of spades.
In the bedroom of his heart he pulled down the shades,

he covered his blood with sackcloth, tried
to think of icebergs, of putrefied

camel flesh. And his face changed seasons
like a speeded-up landscape. He followed his visions

25

to the end of them, growing wiser and warm,
and he knew that her soul's form was like the form

of her supple body, which he soon would embrace—
as a violin's form is the form of its case.

7. *Who Could Stump Whom*

In the pingpong of questions and answers
not a sound was heard
except:
ping . . . pong . . .
And the cough of the learned counselors
and the sharp tearing of paper.

He made black waves with his beard
so that her words would drown in it.
She made a jungle
of her hair, for him to be lost in.
Words were plunked down with a click
like chessmen.
Thoughts with high masts
sailed past one another.
Empty crossword puzzles filled up
as the sky fills with stars,
secret caches were opened,
buckles and vows were unfastened,
cruel religions
were tickled, and laughed
horribly.
In the final game,
her words played with his words, her tongue
with his tongue.
Precise maps
were spread, face up, on the table.
Everything was revealed. Hard.
And pitiless.

8. *The Empty Throne Room*

All the word games
lay scattered out of their boxes.
Boxes were left gaping
after the game.

Sawdust of questions,
shells of cracked parables,
woolly packing materials from
crates of fragile riddles.

Heavy wrapping paper
of love and strategies.
Used solutions rustled
in the trash of thinking.

Long problems
were rolled up on spools,
miracles were locked in their cages.
Chess horses were led back to the stable.

Empty cartons that had
"Handle With Care!"
printed on them
sang hymns of thanksgiving.

Later, in ponderous parade, the King's soldiers arrived.
She fled, sad
as black snakes
in the dry grass.

A moon of atonement spun around the towers
as on Yom Kippur eve.
Caravans with no camels, no people,
no sound, departed and departed and departed.

From In a Right Angle: A Cycle of Quatrains

1

In the sands of prayer my father saw angels' traces.
He saved me a space, but I wandered in other spaces.
That's why his face was bright and why mine is scorched.
Like an old office calendar, I'm covered with times and places.

27

9

I kiss the hem of my fate, as my father would kiss the side
of his prayer-shawl before I would wrap myself deep inside.
I will always remember the free summer clouds and always
the stars that glimmer beyond our need to decide.

13

Along the summer, along the sandy shoreline
of the heart. During the gray stones, at the edge of a lover's incline.
Deep within the black ships, under the grief,
near the steep wish, inside the wind of time.

18

The driver asked. We answered, All the way.
His shoulders said, If that's what you want, okay.
We paid a distant look, a close hello.
Our lives were stamped *To the last stop: one-way.*

24

My love writes commentaries on me, like the rabbis explaining the Bible.
Spring translates the world into every language. On the table
our bread keeps prophesying. Our words are lovely and fresh.
But Fate works inside us overtime, as hard as he's able.

30

I escaped once and don't remember what god it was from, what test.
So I'm floating inside my life, like Jonah in his dark fish, at rest.
I've made a deal with my fish, since we're both in the guts of the world:
I won't get out of him, ever. He'll endure me and not digest.

34

Like torn shirts that my mother couldn't mend,
the dead are strewn about the world. Like them,
we'll never love or know what voices weep
and what winds will pass by to say Amen.

43

Two hopes away from the battle, I had a vision of peace.
My weary head must keep walking, my legs keep dreaming apace.
The scorched man said, I am the bush that burned and that *was* consumed:
come hither, leave your shoes on your feet. This is the place.

45

A young soldier lies in the springtime, cut off from his name.
His body is budding and flowering. From artery and vein
his blood babbles on, uncomprehending and small.
God boils the flesh of the lamb in its mother's pain.

46

In the right angle between a dead man and his mourner I'll start
living from now on, and wait there as it grows dark.
The woman sits with me, the girl in her fiery cloud
rose into the sky, and into my wide-open heart.

As for the World

As for the world,
I am always like one of Socrates' students:
walking beside him,
hearing his seasons and generations,
and all I can do is say:
Yes, certainly that is true.
You are right again.
It is exactly as you have said.

As for my life, I am always
Venice:
everything that is streets
is in other people.
In me—love, dark and flowing.

As for the scream, as for the silence,
I am always a shofar:
hoarding, all year long, its one blast
for the terrible Days of Awe.

As for the deeds,
I am always Cain:
a fugitive and a vagabond before the deed that I won't do,
or after the deed that
can't be undone.

As for the palm of your hand,
as for the signals of my heart
and the plans of my flesh,
as for the writing on the wall,
I am always an ignoramus: I can't
read or write
and my head is empty as a weed,
knowing only the secret whisper
and the motion in the wind
when a fate passes through me, to
some other place.

In the Middle of This Century

In the middle of this century we turned to each other
with half face and full eyes
like an ancient Egyptian painting
and for a short time.

I stroked your hair in a direction opposite to your journey,
we called out to each other
as people call out the names of the cities they don't stop in
along the road.

Beautiful is the world that wakes up early for evil,
beautiful is the world that falls asleep to sin and mercy,
in the profanity of our being together, you and I.
Beautiful is the world.

The earth drinks people and their loves
like wine, in order to forget. It won't be able to.
And like the contours of the Judean mountains,
we also won't find a resting-place.

In the middle of this century we turned to each other.
I saw your body, casting the shadow, waiting for me.
The leather straps of a long journey
had long since been tightened crisscross on my chest.
I spoke in praise of your mortal loins,

you spoke in praise of my transient face,
I stroked your hair in the direction of your journey,
I touched the tidings of your last day,
I touched your hand that has never slept,
I touched your mouth that now, perhaps, will sing.

Desert dust covered the table
we hadn't eaten from.
But with my finger I wrote in it the letters of your name.

Farewell,

face of you, already face of dreaming.
Wandering rises up, aloft and wild.
Face of beasts, of water, face of leaving,
grove of whispers, face of breast, of child.

No more the hour in which we two could happen,
no more for us to murmur: *now* and *all*.
You had a name of wind and raincloud, woman
of tensions and intentions, mirror, fall.

For what we didn't know, we sang together.
Changes and generations, face of night.
No longer mine, code unresolved forever,
closed-nippled, buckled, mouthed and twisted tight.

And so farewell to you, who will not slumber,
for all was in our words, a world of sand.
From this day forth, you turn into the dreamer
of everything: the world within your hand.

Farewell, death's bundles, suitcase packed with waiting.
Threads, feathers, holy chaos. Hair held fast.
For look: what will not be, no hand is writing;
and what was not the body's will not last.

Such as Sorrow

Should you realize so much, daughter of every season,
this year's fading flowers or last year's snow.
And afterward, not for us, not the vial of poison,
but rather the cup and the muteness and the long way to go.

Like two briefcases we were interchanged for each other.
Now I am no longer I, and you are not you.
No more returning, no more approaching together,
just a candle snuffed in the wine, as when Sabbath is through.

Now all that's left from your sun is the pallid moon.
Trivial words that may comfort today or tomorrow:
Such as, give me rest. Such as, let it all go and be gone.
Such as, come and hand me my last hour. Such as, sorrow.

Jerusalem

On a roof in the Old City
laundry hanging in the late afternoon sunlight:
the white sheet of a woman who is my enemy,
the towel of a man who is my enemy,
to wipe off the sweat of his brow.

In the sky of the Old City
a kite.
At the other end of the string,
a child
I can't see
because of the wall.

We have put up many flags,
they have put up many flags.
To make us think that they're happy.
To make them think that we're happy.

Before

Before the gate has been closed,
before the last question is posed,
before I am transposed.
Before the weeds fill the gardens,
before there are no more pardons,
before the concrete hardens.
Before all the flute-holes are covered,
before things are locked in the cupboard,
before the rules are discovered.
Before the conclusion is planned,
before God closes his hand,
before we have nowhere to stand.

And as Far as Abu Ghosh

And as far as Abu Ghosh we were silent
and as far as old age I will love you
at the foot of the hill of horrors,
in the den of the winds. And in Sha'ar Ha-Gai
the angels of the three religions stepped down into
the road. Faith in one god is still heavy. And with words
of pain I must describe the fig trees
and what happened to me, which wasn't my fault. Sand
was blown into my eyes and became tears. And in Ramla
small planes were parked, and large nameless dead. The scent
of orange groves touched my blood. My blood looked
over its shoulder to see who touched. Winds, like actors, began
to put on their costumes again so that they could act before us,
their masks of house and mountain and woods,
makeup of sunset and night.

From there the other roads began.
And my heart was covered with dreams, like my shiny
shoes, which were covered with dust.
For dreams too are a long road
whose end I will never reach.

You Too Got Tired

You too got tired of being an advertisement
for our world, so that angels could see: yes it's pretty, earth.
Relax. Take a rest from smiling. And without complaint
allow the sea-breeze to lift the corners of your mouth.

You won't object; your eyes too, like flying paper,
are flying. The fruit has fallen from the sycamore tree.
How do you say *to love* in the dialect of water?
In the language of earth, what part of speech are we?

Here is the street. What sense does it finally make:
any mound, a last wind. What prophet would sing. . . .
And at night, from out of my sleep, you begin to talk.
And how shall I answer you. And what shall I bring.

The Place Where We Are Right

From the place where we are right
flowers will never grow
in the spring.

The place where we are right
is hard and trampled
like a yard.

But doubts and loves
dig up the world
like a mole, a plow.
And a whisper will be heard in the place
where the ruined
house once stood.

Mayor

It's sad to be
the mayor of Jerusalem—
it's terrible.
How can a man be mayor of such a city?
What can he do with it?
Build and build and build.

And at night the stones of the mountains crawl down
and surround the stone houses,
like wolves coming to howl at the dogs,
who have become the slaves of men.

Resurrection

Afterward they will get up
all together, and with a sound of chairs scraping
they will face the narrow exit.

And their clothes are crumpled
and covered with dust and cigarette ashes
and their hand discovers in the inside pocket
a ticket stub from a very previous season.

And their faces are still crisscrossed
with God's will.
And their eyes are red from so much sleeplessness
under the ground.

And right away, questions:
What time is it?
Where did you put mine?
When? When?

And one of them can be seen in an ancient
scanning of the sky, to see if rain.
Or a woman,

with an age-old gesture, wipes her eyes
and lifts the heavy hair
at the back of her neck.

From Summer or Its End

You washed the fruit.
You murdered the bacteria.
On the chair: a watch and a dress.
In the bed: us,
without any of these
and each for the other.
And if it weren't for our names
we would have been completely naked.

It was marvelous, the dream on
the table.
We left the fruit
forever till the next day.
And one of these evenings
I'll have a lot to say about
everything that remains and is kept inside us.

After midnight, when our words began
to influence the world,
I put my hand on your forehead:
your thoughts were smaller than the palm of my hand,
but I knew this was a mistake,
like the mistake of the hand that covers
the sun.

              ¤

Last to dry was the hair.
When we were already far from the sea,
when words and salt, which had merged on us,
separated from one another with a sigh,
and your body no longer showed
signs of a terrible ancientness.
And in vain we had forgotten a few things on the beach,

so that we would have an excuse to return.
We didn't return.

And these days I remember the days
that have your name on them, like a name on a ship,
and how we saw through two open doors
one man who was thinking, and how we looked at the clouds
with the ancient gaze we inherited from our fathers,
who waited for rain,
and how at night, when the world cooled off,
your body kept its warmth for a long time,
like the sea.

                    ¤

Like the imprint of our bodies,
not a sign will remain that we were here.
The world closes behind us,
the sand is smoothed out again.
And already on the calendar there are dates
you will no longer exist in,
already a wind bringing clouds
that won't rain on us.

And your name is on the passenger list of
ships and in the guest books
of hotels whose very names
deaden the heart.

The three languages that I know,
all the colors that I see and dream,
won't help me.

                    ¤

If with a bitter mouth you speak
sweet words, the world will not grow sweet
and will not grow bitter.

And it is written in the book that we shall not fear.
And it is written that we too shall change,
like the words,
in future and in past,
in plural and in loneliness.

And soon, in the coming nights,
we will appear, like wandering actors,
each in the other's dream
and in the dreams of strangers whom we didn't know together.

In the Full Severity of Mercy

Count them.
You are able to count them. They
are not like the sand on the seashore. They
are not innumerable like the stars. They are like lonely people.
On the corner or in the street.

Count them. See them
seeing the sky through ruined houses.
Go out through the stones and come back. What
will you come back to? But count them, for they
do their time in dreams
and they walk around outside and their hopes are unbandaged
and gaping, and they will die of them.

Count them.
Too soon they learned to read the terrible
writing on the wall. To read and write on
other walls. And the feast continues in silence.

Count them. Be present, for they
have already used up all the blood and there's still not enough,
as in a dangerous operation, when one
is exhausted and beaten like ten thousand. For who is
the judge, and what is the judgment,
unless it be in the full sense of the night
and in the full severity of mercy.

Too Many

Too many olive trees in the valley,
too many stones on the slope.
Too many dead, too little
earth to cover them all.
And I must return to the landscapes painted
on the bank notes
and to my father's face on the coins.

Too many memorial days, too little
remembering. My friends have
forgotten what they learned when they were young.
And my girlfriend lies in a hidden place
and I am always outside, food for hungry winds.
Too much weariness, too few eyes
to contain it. Too many clocks,
too little time. Too many oaths
on the Bible, too many highways, too few
ways where we can truly go: each to his destiny.
Too many hopes
that ran away from their masters.
Too many dreamers. Too few dreams
whose interpretation would change the history of the world
like Pharaoh's dreams.

My life closes behind me. And I am outside, a dog
for the cruel, blind wind that always
pushes at my back. I am well trained: I rise and sit
and wait to lead it through the streets
of my life, which could have been my true life.

Poem for Arbor Day

Children are planting their shoots
that will become the forest
they'll get lost in, terribly, when they grow up.

And they count with numbers
that will shatter their whole nights

to make them illuminated and outside,
sleepless, yearless.

The almond tree is in bloom
and it smells the smell of
humans as they walk
in the sweat of the fear of their living
for the first time.

And their voice will carry their joy, like a porter who carries
an expensive chair, not his, to the strange house,
and puts it down there in the rooms
and leaves, alone.

Jacob and the Angel

Just before dawn she sighed and held him
that way, and defeated him.
And he held her that way, and defeated her,
and both of them knew that a hold
brings death.
They agreed to do without names.

But in the first light
he saw her body,
which remained white in the places
the swimsuit had covered, yesterday.

Then someone called her suddenly from above,
twice.
The way you call a little girl from playing
in the yard.
And he knew her name; and let her go.

Here

Here, underneath the kites that the children are flying
and the ones the telephone lines snatched last year, I stand
with the strong branches of my quiet decisions that have
long since grown from me and the birds of the small hesitation
in my heart and the boulders of the huge hesitation at my feet
and my two twin eyes, one of which is always
busy and the other always in love. And my gray pants
and my green sweater, and my face absorbing colors
and reflecting colors; and I don't know what else
I return and receive and project and reject
and how I was a market for many things.
Import-export. Border checkpoint. Crossroads.
Division of waters, of the dead. The meeting-place. The parting-place.

And the wind comes through a treetop and lingers
in every leaf; but still,
how it passes without stopping
while we come and stay a little and then fall.
And as between sisters, there is much resemblance between us and the world:
thighs and mountainside. A distant thought
looks like the deed that grew here in the flesh and on the mountain,
looks like the cypresses that happened, dark, in the mountain range.
The circle closes. I am its buckle.

And before I discovered that my hard fathers
are soft on the inside, they died.
And all the generations that came before me are many acrobats
mounted on one another in the circus,
and usually I am the one on the bottom
while all of them, a heavy load, stand on my shoulders,
and sometimes I am on the top: one hand lifted
to the roof; and the applause in the arena below
is my flesh and my reward.

Elegy on an Abandoned Village

1

The wine of August was spilled on the face of the girl, but
the destruction was sober. Thick wooden beams stuck out
from the life of forgotten people; and a distant love
hurled itself, echoing like thunder, into the ravine.
And slowly the valleys rose to the mountain, in the midday
hours, and we were almost sad. And like some stranger
in a strange city, who reads in a book of addresses and names,
I stand and choose a hotel, temporary: here.

2

The enormous snow was set down far away. Sometimes
I must use my love as the only way to describe it,
and must hire the wind to demonstrate the wailing of women.
It's hard for stones that roll from season to season
to remember the dreamers and the whisperers in the grass,
who fell in their love. And like a man who keeps shaking
his wrist when his watch stops: Who is shaking us? Who?

3

The wind brought voices from far away, like an infant
in her arms. The wind never stops. There, standing,
are the power-plants that discovered our weakness when
we needed to appear strong, needed to make
a decision in the dark, without a mirror or a light.

Thoughts have dropped and fly parallel to the ground, like birds.
And beside the sea: picnickers sit among friends.
Their money was brought from far away; their portrait is seen
on crumpling paper. In their laughter: blossoming clouds.
Our heart beats in the footsteps that watchmen take, back and forth.
And if someone should love us, surely the distant snow
will realize it, a long time before we do.

4

The rest is not simply silence. The rest is a screech.
Like a car shifting gears on a dangerous uphill road.
Have you listened closely enough to the calls of the children
at play in the ruined houses, when their voices stop

short, as they reach the ceiling, out of habit, and later
burst up to the sky? Oh night without a Jerusalem,
oh children in the ruins, who will never again be birds,
oh passing time, when newspapers that have yellowed already
interest you again: like a document. And the face of last year's
woman lights up in the memory of a distant man.
But the wind keeps forgetting. Because it is always there.

Should I wait here for God's voice, or for the scream of a train
between the hard-pressing hills? Look, children and birds
were closed and opened, each into song and muteness.
Or girls on their long road: look as again they turn into
fig trees; how wonderful they are for love. And the thunder
of sparrows as they rise from the garbage; see what is written
on stones. You weren't the one who wrote it. And yet
it is always your handwriting. Stay for a while, in the narrow
place between earth and its short god. Listen as the tin
gradually matures in its rust, and the voice of alleys
changes too late: not till death has arrived.

For only in the half-destroyed do we understand
the blue that covers the inside of rooms, like doctors
who learn by the bodies gaping in front of them. But we
will never know how blood behaves when it's inside,
within the whole body, when the heart shines into it, from
far away, in its dark path. And girls are still
hidden among the fresh laundry hanging in the air
that also will turn into rain among the mountains
sent to scout and uncover the nakedness of the land;
and uncovered it; and stayed in the valleys, forever.

The Elegy on the Lost Child

I can see by their mark how high the waters reached
last winter; but how can I know what level
love reached inside me? And perhaps it overflowed my banks.
For what remained in the wadi?—just congealed mud.
What remained on my face?—not even a thin white line,
as above the lips of the child who was drinking milk

and put down the glass, with a click, on the kitchen table.
What remained? Perhaps a leaf in the small
stone that was placed on the windowsill, to watch over us
like an angel when we were inside. And to love means not
to remain; means not to leave a trace, but to change
utterly. To be forgotten. And to understand means to bloom.
Spring understands. To remember the belovèd means to
forget the many belongings that piled up.
Loving means having to forget the other love,
closing the other doors. Look, we saved a seat,
we put down a coat or a book on the empty chair
next to us, perhaps empty forever. And how long
could we keep it for ourselves? After all, someone will come,
a stranger will sit beside you. And you turn around,
impatient, to the door with the red sign over it, you look
at your watch; that too is a habit of prayer, like bowing
and kissing. And outside they always invent new thoughts
and these too are placed on the tired faces of people,
like colored lights in the street. Or look at the child, whose
thoughts are painted upon him like a pattern upon
an ancient urn, for others to see, he still isn't
thinking them for himself. The earth wanders, passes
beneath the soles of our shoes, like a moving stage,
like your face which I thought was mine and wasn't. But the child
got lost. The last scion of his games, the Benjamin
of colored paper, the grandson of his ancient hiding-places.
He came and went in the ringing of his toys among
empty wells, at the ends of holidays and within
the terrible cycle of cries and silence, in the process
of hope and death and hope. Everyone searched,
they were happy to look for some thing in the land of forgetting:
voices and a plane flying low like thoughts, police dogs
with philosophers' faces, question-words hopping on thin legs
in the grass that gets drier and drier, before our very
eyes. Words worn out from prayers and talk and newspapers,
prophecies of Jeremiah down on all fours.

And in the big cities, protesters blocked the roads like
a blocked heart, whose master will die. And the dead were already
hung out like fruit, for eternal ripening within
the history of the world. They searched for the child; and found
pairs of lovers, hidden; found ancient urns;

found everything that sought *not* to be revealed. For love
was too short and didn't cover them all, like a too-short
blanket. A head or two feet stuck out in the wind
when the cold night came. Or they found a short-cut of sharp
brief pain instead of the long, oblivion-causing
streets of joy and of satiation. And at night
the names of the world, of foreign cities and dark
lakes and peoples long vanished. And all the names
are like my belovèd's name. She lifted her head
to listen. She had the feeling that she had been called,
and she wasn't the one we meant. But the child disappeared
and the paths in the distant mountain emerged. Not much time.
The olives spoke hard stones. In the enormous fear
between heaven and earth, new houses arose and the glass
of windowpanes cooled the burning forehead of night.
The hot wind pounced upon us from a thicket of dry grass,
the distraction of mutual need erected high bridges
in the wasteland. Traps were set, spotlights turned on,
and nets of woven hair were spread out. But they passed
the place, and didn't see, for the child bent over
and hid in the stones of tomorrow's houses. Eternal
paper rustled between the feet of the searchers.
Printed and unprinted. The orders were clearly heard.
Exact numbers: not ten or fifty or a hundred.
But twenty-seven, thirty-one, forty-three, so that they would believe us.

And in the morning the search was renewed: quick, here!
I saw him among the toys of his wells, the games
of his stones, the tools of his olive trees. I heard his heartbeat
under the rock. He's there. He's here. And the tree
stirs. Did you all see? And new calls, like an ancient
sea bringing new ships with loud calls to the foreign shore.
We returned to our cities, where a great sorrow is divided among them
at appropriate intervals, like mailboxes, so that we can drop ours
into them: name and address, times of pickup. And the stones
chanted in the choir of black mouths, into the earth,
and only the child could hear them; we couldn't. For he stayed
longer than we did, pretending from the clouds and already
known by heart to the children of olive trees,
familiar and changing and not leaving a trace, as in love,
and belonged to them completely, without a remnant.
For to love means not to remain. To be forgotten. But God

remembers, like a man who returns to the place he once left
to reclaim a memory he needed. Thus God returns to
our small room, so that he can remember how much he wanted
to build his creation with love. And he didn't forget
our names. Names aren't forgotten. We call a shirt
shirt: even when it's used as a dustrag, it's still called *shirt*,
perhaps *the old shirt.* And how long will we go on like this?
For we are changing. But the name remains. And what right
do we have to be called by our names, or to call the Jordan
Jordan after it has passed through the Sea of Galilee
and has come out at Zemach. Who is it? Is it still the one
that entered at Capernaum? Who are we after we pass through
the terrible love? Who is the Jordan? Who
remembers? Rowboats have emerged. The mountains are mute:
Susita, Hermon, the terrifying Arbel, painful Tiberias.

We all turn our backs on names, the rules of the game,
the hollow calls. An hour passes, hair is cut off
in the barbershop. The door is opened. What remains is for
the broom and the street. And the barber's watch ticking close to
your ear as he bends over you. This too is time.
Time's end, perhaps. The child hasn't been found.
The results of rain are seen even now when it's summer.
Aloud the trees are talking from the sleep of the earth.
Voices made out of tin are ringing in the wind
as it wakes up. We lay together. I walked away:
the belovèd's eyes stayed wide open in fear. She sat up
in bed for a while, leaning on her elbows. The sheet
was white like the day of judgment, and she couldn't stay
alone in the house, she went out into the world
that began with the stairs near the door. But the child remained
and began to resemble the mountains and the winds and the trunks
of olive trees. A family resemblance: as the face of a young man
who fell in the Negev arises in the face of his cousin
born in New York. The fracture of a mountain in the Aravah
reappears in the face of the shattered friend. Mountain range
and night, resemblance and tradition. Night's custom that turned
into the law of lovers. Temporary precautions
became permanent. The police, the calls outside, the speaking
inside the bodies. And the fire-engines don't wail when they come from
the fire. Silently they return from embers and ashes.
Silently we returned from the valley after love and searching
in retrospect: not being paid attention to. But a few of us

continued to listen. It seemed as if someone was calling.
We extended the outer ear with the palm of a hand,
we extended the area of the heart with a further love
in order to hear more clearly, in order to forget.

But the child died in the night
clean and well groomed. Neat and licked by the tongues
of God and night. "When we got here, it was still daylight.
Now darkness has come." Clean and white like a sheet of
paper in an envelope closed and chanted upon
in the psalm-books of the lands of the dead. A few went on searching,
or perhaps they searched for a pain that would fit their tears,
for a joy that would fit their laughter, though nothing can fit
anything else. Even hands are from a different body.
But it seemed to us that something had fallen. We heard
a ringing, like a coin that fell. We stood for a moment.
We turned around. We bent down. We didn't find
anything, and we went on walking. Each to his own.

Jerusalem, 1967

To my friends Dennis, Arieh, and Harold

1
This year I traveled a long way
to view the silence of my city.
A baby calms down when you rock it, a city calms down
from the distance. I dwelled in longing. I played the hopscotch
of the four strict squares of Yehuda Ha-Levi:
My heart. Myself. East. West.

I heard bells ringing in the religions of time,
but the wailing that I heard inside me
has always been from my Yehudean desert.

Now that I've come back, I'm screaming again.
And at night, stars rise like the bubbles of the drowned,
and every morning I scream the scream of a newborn baby
at the tumult of houses and at all this huge light.

2

I've come back to this city where names
are given to distances as if to human beings
and the numbers are not of bus routes
but: 70 After, 1917, 500
B.C., Forty-eight. These are the lines
you really travel on.

And already the demons of the past are meeting
with the demons of the future and negotiating about me
above me, their give-and-take neither giving nor taking,
in the high arches of shell-orbits above my head.

A man who comes back to Jerusalem is aware that the places
that used to hurt don't hurt anymore.
But a light warning remains in everything,
like the movement of a light veil: warning.

3

Illuminated is the Tower of David, illuminated is the Church of Maria,
illuminated the patriarchs sleeping in their burial cave, illuminated
are the faces from inside, illuminated the translucent
honey cakes, illuminated the clock and illuminated the time
passing through your thighs as you take off your dress.

Illuminated illuminated. Illuminated are the cheeks of my childhood,
illuminated the stones that wanted to be illuminated
along with those that wanted to sleep in the darkness of squares.

Illuminated are the spiders of the banister and the cobwebs of churches
and the acrobats of the stairs. But more than all these, and in them all,
illuminated is the terrible, true X-ray writing
in letters of bones, in white and lightning: *MENE*
MENE TEKEL UPHARSIN.

4

In vain you will look for the fences of barbed wire.
You know that such things
don't disappear. A different city perhaps
is now being cut in two; two lovers
separated; a different flesh is tormenting itself now
with these thorns, refusing to be stone.

In vain you will look. You lift up your eyes unto the hills,
perhaps there? Not these hills, accidents of geology,
but The Hills. You ask
questions without a rise in your voice, without a question mark,
only because you're supposed to ask them; and they
don't exist. But a great weariness wants you with all your might
and gets you. Like death.

Jerusalem, the only city in the world
where the right to vote is granted even to the dead.

5
On Yom Kippur in 1967, the Year of Forgetting, I put on
my dark holiday clothes and walked to the Old City of Jerusalem.
For a long time I stood in front of an Arab's hole-in-the-wall shop,
not far from the Damascus Gate, a shop with
buttons and zippers and spools of thread
in every color and snaps and buckles.
A rare light and many colors, like an open Ark.

I told him in my heart that my father too
had a shop like this, with thread and buttons.
I explained to him in my heart about all the decades
and the causes and the events, why I am now here
and my father's shop was burned there and he is buried here.

When I finished, it was time for the Closing of the Gates prayer.
He too lowered the shutters and locked the gate
and I returned, with all the worshipers, home.

6
It's not time that keeps me far away from my childhood,
it's this city and everything in it. Now
I've got to learn Arabic too, to reach all the way to Jericho
from both ends of time; and the length of walls has been added
and the height of towers and the domes of prayer houses
whose area is immeasurable. All these
really broaden my life and force me
always to emigrate once more from the smell
of river and forest.

49

My life is stretched out this way; it grows very thin
like cloth, transparent. You can see right through me.

7
In this summer of wide-open-eyed hatred
and blind love, I'm beginning to believe again
in all the little things that will fill
the holes left by the shells: soil, a bit of grass,
perhaps, after the rains, small insects of every kind.
I think of children growing up half in the ethics of their fathers
and half in the science of war.
The tears now penetrate into my eyes from the outside
and my ears invent, every day, the footsteps of
the messenger of good tidings.

8
The city plays hide-and-seek among her names:
Yerushalayim, Al-Quds, Salem, Jeru, Yeru, all the while
whispering her first, Jebusite name: Y'vus,
Y'vus, Y'vus, in the dark. She weeps
with longing: Ælia Capitolina, Ælia, Ælia.
She comes to any man who calls her
at night, alone. But we know
who comes to whom.

9
On an open door a sign hangs: Closed.
How do you explain it? Now
the chain is free at both ends: there is no
prisoner and no warden, no dog and no master.
The chain will gradually turn into wings.
How do you explain it?
Ah well, you'll explain it.

10
Jerusalem is short and crouched among its hills,
unlike New York, for example.
Two thousand years ago she crouched
in the marvelous starting-line position.
All the other cities ran ahead, did long
laps in the arena of time, they won or lost,
and died. Jerusalem remained in the starting-crouch:

all the victories are clenched inside her,
hidden inside her. All the defeats.
Her strength grows and her breathing is calm
for a race even beyond the arena.

11
Loneliness is always in the middle,
protected and fortified. People were supposed
to feel secure in that, and they don't.
When they go out, after a long time,
caves are formed for the new solitaries.
What do you know about Jerusalem.
You don't need to understand languages;
they pass through everything as if through the ruins of houses.
People are a wall of moving stones.
But even in the Wailing Wall
I haven't seen stones as sad as these.
The letters of my pain are illuminated
like the name of the hotel across the street.
What awaits me and what doesn't await me.

12
Jerusalem stone is the only stone that can
feel pain. It has a network of nerves.
From time to time Jerusalem crowds into
mass protests like the tower of Babel.
But with huge clubs God-the-Police beats her
down: houses are razed, walls flattened,
and afterward the city disperses, muttering
prayers of complaint and sporadic screams from churches
and synagogues and loud-moaning mosques.
Each to his own place.

13
Always beside ruined houses and iron girders
twisted like the arms of the slain, you find
someone who is sweeping the paved path
or tending the little garden, sensitive
paths, square flower-beds.
Large desires for a horrible death are well cared-for
as in the monastery of the White Brothers next to the Lions' Gate.
But farther on, in the courtyard, the earth gapes:

columns and arches supporting vain land
and negotiating with one another: crusaders and guardian angels,
a sultan and Rabbi Yehuda the Pious. Arched vaults with a
column, ransom for prisoners, and strange conditions in rolled-up
contracts, and sealing-stones. Curved hooks holding
air.
Capitals and broken pieces of columns scattered like chessmen
in a game that was interrupted in anger,
and Herod, who already, two thousand years ago, wailed
like mortar shells. He knew.

14
If clouds are a ceiling, I would like to
sit in the room beneath them: a dead kingdom rises
up from me, up, like steam from hot food.
A door squeaks: an opening cloud.
In the distances of valleys someone rapped iron against stone
but the echo erects large, different things in the air.

Above the houses—houses with houses above them. This is
all of history.
This learning in schools without roof
and without walls and without chairs and without teachers.
This learning in the absolute outside,
a learning short as a single heartbeat. All of it.

15
I and Jerusalem are like a blind man and a cripple.
She sees for me
out to the Dead Sea, to the End of Days.
And I hoist her up on my shoulders
and walk blind in my darkness underneath.

16
On this bright autumn day
I establish Jerusalem once again.
The foundation scrolls
are flying in the air, birds, thoughts.

God is angry with me
because I always force him
to create the world once again

from chaos, light, second day, until
man, and back to the beginning.

17

In the morning the shadow of the Old City falls
on the New. In the afternoon—vice versa.
Nobody profits. The muezzin's prayer
is wasted on the new houses. The ringing
bells roll like balls and bounce back.
The shout of *Holy, Holy, Holy* from the synagogues will fade
like gray smoke.

At the end of summer I breathe this air
that is burnt and pained. My thoughts have
the stillness of many closed books:
many crowded books, with most of their pages
stuck together like eyelids in the morning.

18

I climb up the Tower of David
a little higher than the prayer that ascends the highest:
halfway to heaven. A few of
the ancients succeeded: Mohammed, Jesus,
and others. Though they didn't find rest in heaven;
they just entered a higher excitement. But
the applause for them hasn't stopped ever since,
down below.

19

Jerusalem is built on the vaulted foundations
of a held-back scream. If there were no reason
for the scream, the foundations would crumble, the city would collapse;
if the scream were screamed, Jerusalem would explode into the heavens.

20

Poets come in the evening into the Old City
and they emerge from it pockets stuffed with images
and metaphors and little well-constructed parables
and crepuscular similes from among columns and crypts,
from within darkening fruit
and delicate filigree of hammered hearts.

I lifted my hand to my forehead
to wipe off the sweat
and found I had accidentally raised up
the ghost of Else Lasker-Schüler.
Light and tiny as she was
in her life, all the more so in her death. Ah, but
her poems.

21
Jerusalem is a port city on the shore of eternity.
The Temple Mount is a huge ship, a magnificent
luxury liner. From the portholes of her Western Wall
cheerful saints look out, travelers. Hasidim on the pier
wave goodbye, shout hooray, hooray, bon voyage! She is
always arriving, always sailing away. And the fences and the piers
and the policemen and the flags and the high masts of churches
and mosques and the smokestacks of synagogues and the boats
of psalms of praise and the mountain-waves. The shofar blows: another one
has just left. Yom Kippur sailors in white uniforms
climb among ladders and ropes of well-tested prayers.

And the commerce and the gates and the golden domes:
Jerusalem is the Venice of God.

22
Jerusalem is Sodom's sister-city,
but the merciful salt didn't have mercy on her
and didn't cover her with a silent whiteness.
Jerusalem is an unconsenting Pompeii.
History books that were thrown into the fire,
their pages are strewn about, stiffening in red.

An eye whose color is too light, blind,
always shattered in a sieve of veins.
Many births gaping below,
a womb with numberless teeth,
a double-edged woman and the holy beasts.

The sun thought that Jerusalem was a sea
and set in her: a terrible mistake.
Sky fish were caught in a net of alleys,
tearing one another to pieces.

Jerusalem. An operation that was left open.
The surgeons went to take a nap in faraway skies,
but her dead gradually
formed a circle, all around her,
like quiet petals.
My God.
My stamen.
Amen.

The Bull Returns

The bull returns from his day of work in the ring
after a cup of coffee with his opponents,
having left them a note with his address and
the exact location of the red scarf.
The sword remains in his stiff-necked neck.
And when he's usually at home. Now
he sits on his bed, with his heavy
Jewish eyes. He knows
that the sword too is hurt when it pierces flesh.
In his next incarnation he'll be a sword: the hurt will remain.
("The door is open. If not, the key is under
the mat.")
He knows about the mercy of twilight and about the final
mercy. In the Bible, he's listed with the clean animals.
He's very kosher: chews his cud,
and even his heart is divided and cloven like a hoof.
From his chest, hairs burst forth
dry and gray, as though from a split mattress.

A Luxury

My uncle is buried at Sheikh Badr, my other uncle
is scattered in the Carpathians, my father is buried in Sanhedria,
my grandmother on the Mount of Olives, and all their forefathers
are buried in a half-destroyed Jewish graveyard

among the villages of Lower Franconia,
near rivers and forests that are not Jerusalem.

Grandfather, Grandfather, who converted heavy-eyed cows
in his barn underneath the kitchen and got up at four in the morning.
I inherited this earliness from him. With a mouth
bitter from nightmares, I go out to feed my bad dreams.

Grandfather, Grandfather, chief rabbi of my life,
sell my pains the way you used to sell
khametz on Passover eve: so that they stay in me and even go on hurting
but won't be mine. Won't belong to me.

So many tombstones are scattered in the past of my life,
engraved names like the names of stations
where the train doesn't stop any more.

How will I cover all the distances on my own routes,
how will I make connections among them all? I can't afford
to maintain such an expensive railway system. It's a luxury.

To Bake the Bread of Yearning

The last time I went to see my child
he was still eating pablum. Now, sadly,
bread and meat, with knife and fork,
with manners that are already preparing him
to die quietly, politely.

He thinks I'm a sailor, knows I don't have a ship
or a sea; only great distances and winds.
The movements of my father's body in prayer
and mine in lovemaking
are already folded in his small body.

To be an adult means
to bake the bread of yearning
all night long, with reddened face
in front of the fire. My child sees.

And the powerful spell *See you soon*
which he's learned to say
works only among the dead.

National Thoughts

A woman, caught in a homeland-trap of the Chosen People: you.
Cossack's fur hat on your head: you the
offspring of their pogroms. "After these things had come to pass,"
always.
Or, for example, your face: slanting eyes,
eyes descended from massacre. High cheekbones
of a hetman, head of murderers.
But a mitzvah dance of Hasidim,
naked on a rock at twilight,
beside the water canopies of Ein Gedi,
with eyes closed and body open like hair. After
these things had come to pass. "Always."

People caught in a homeland-trap:
to speak now in this weary language,
a language that was torn from its sleep in the Bible: dazzled,
it wobbles from mouth to mouth. In a language that once described
miracles and God, to say car, bomb, God.

Square letters want to stay
closed; each letter a closed house,
to stay and to close yourself in
and to sleep inside it, forever.

A Pity. We Were Such a Good Invention

They amputated
your thighs from my hips.
As far as I'm concerned, they're always
doctors. All of them.

They dismantled us
from each other. As far as I'm concerned,
they're engineers.
A pity. We were such a good and loving
invention: an airplane made of a man and a woman,
wings and all:
we even got off
the ground a little.
We even flew.

Elegy

The wind won't come to draw smiles in the sand of dreams.
The wind will be strong.
And people are walking without flowers,
unlike their children in the festival of the first fruits.
And a few of them are victors and most of them are vanquished,
passing through the arch of others' victories
and as on the Arch of Titus everything appears, in bas-relief:
the warm and belovèd bed, the faithful and much-scrubbed pot,
and the lamp, not the one with the seven branches, but the simple one,
the good one, which didn't fail even on winter nights,
and the table, a domestic animal that stands on four legs and keeps
    silent. . . .
And they are brought into the arena to fight with wild beasts
and they see the heads of the spectators in the stadium
and their courage is like the crying of their children,
persistent, persistent and ineffectual.
And in their back pocket, letters are rustling,
and the victors put the words into their mouths
and if they sing, it is not their own song,
and the victors set large yearnings inside them
like loaves of dough
and they bake these in their love
and the victors will eat the warm bread and *they* won't.

But a bit of their love remains on them
like the primitive decorations on ancient urns:
the first, modest line of emotion all around

and then the swirl of dreams
and then two parallel lines,
mutual love,
or a pattern of small flowers, a memory of childhood, high-stalked
and thin-legged.

Threading

Loving each other began this way: threading
loneliness into loneliness
patiently, our hands trembling and precise.

Longing for the past gave our eyes
the double security of what won't change
and of what can't be returned to.

But the heart must kill one of us
on one of its forays,
if not you—me,
when it comes back empty-handed,
like Cain, a boomerang from the field.

Now in the Storm

Now in the storm before the calm
I can tell you what
in the calm before the storm I didn't say
because they would have heard us and discovered our hiding-place.

That we were just neighbors in the fierce wind,
brought together in the ancient *khamsin* from Mesopotamia.
And the Latter Prophets of my veins' kingdom
prophesied into the firmament of your flesh.

And the weather was good for us and for the heart,
and the sun's muscles were flexed inside us and golden

in the Olympiad of emotions, on the faces of thousands of spectators,
so that we would know, and remain, and there would again be clouds.

Look, we met in a protected place, in the angle
where history began to arise, quiet
and safe from all the hasty events.
And the voice began to tell stories in the evening, by the children's bed.

And now it's too early for archaeology
and too late to repair what has been done.
Summer will arrive, and the *clop, clop* of the hard sandals
will sink in the soft sand, forever.

Travels of the Last Benjamin of Tudela

You ate and were filled, you came
in your twelfth year, in the Thirties
of the world, with short pants that reached down to your knees,
tassels dangling from your undershawl
sticky between your legs in the sweltering land.
Your skin still smooth, without protective hair.
The brown, round eyes you had, according
to the pattern of ripe cherries, will get used to
oranges. Orange scents. Innocence.
Clocks were set, according
to the beats of the round heart, train tracks
according to the capacity of children's feet.

And silently, like a doctor and mother, the days bent over me
and started to whisper to one another, while the grass
already was laid flat by the bitter wind
on the slope of hills I will never walk on again.
Moon and stars and ancient deeds of grownups
were placed on a high shelf beyond
my arm's reach;
and I stood in vain underneath the forbidden bookshelves.
But even then I was marked for annihilation like an orange scored
for peeling, like chocolate, like a hand-grenade for explosion and death.
The hand of fate held me, aimed. My skies were the

inside of the soft palm wrapped around me, and on the outside:
rough skin, hard stars, protruding veins,
airplane routes, black hairs, mortar-shell trajectories
in silence or in wailing, in black or in radiant flares.
And before I was real and lingering here
the heart's shoulders carried an anguish not mine
and from somewhere else ideas entered, slowed-down
and with a deep rumble, like a train
into the hollow, listening station.

You ate and were filled and recited the blessing
alone and in company and alone.
In the bridal chamber after the wedding, and outside
the bearded witnesses stood and listened
to the sounds of love, to the sighs and murmurs and screams,
mine and yours, in that room. And at the door
wedding gifts piled up like gifts for the
dead at the mouth of the Pharaohs' tombs.
Stone lions from the bridges of my childhood city watched over us
along with stone lions from the old house in Jerusalem.

You didn't eat, weren't filled. You spoke big words
with a small mouth. Your heart will never learn to judge distances.
The farthest distance it knows is the nearest tree,
the curb of the sidewalk, the face of the belovèd. Like a blind man,
the blind heart hit against the obstacle with its cane and it still
hits and gropes, without advancing. Hits and will hit.
Loneliness is one of the tenses in which an action's time
can be conjugated: hits, will hit. Time is a fragrance. For example,
the fragrance of 1929, when sorrow recited over you the blessing
of the first fruits. And you didn't know that you
were her first fruit.

You were educated in a Montessori kindergarten. They taught you
to love doing things alone, with your very own hands,
they educated you for loneliness. You masturbated
in secret: nocturnal emissions, diurnal additions. "I'll tell your father."
Rosh Hashanah halls echoey and hollow, and white
Yom Kippur machines made of bright metal, cogwheels
of prayers, a conveyor belt of prostrations and bows
with a menacing buzz. You have sinned, you have gone astray
inside a dark womb shaped like the dome of a synagogue,

61

the round, primordial cave of prayer,
the holy ark, gaping open, blinded you
in a third-degree interrogation. Do you confess? Do you confess?
I confess before Thee in the morning with the sun out. What's
your name? Do you surrender? You have transgressed, you are guilty, are you
    alive?
How do you? ("Do you love me?") You have remembered, you have forgotten.

Oh Montessori, Montessori, with your white hair,
the first dead woman that I loved. "Hey kid!" Even now
I turn around in the street if I hear that
behind me.
Slowly and with terrible pains the I turns into a he, after
resting a little in the you. You turns into they. The surgery is performed
with open eyes, only the place is anesthetized with ice perhaps
or with a love pill. After you too they will call: Dreamer! Dreamer!
You won't be able to. What's your name now? And not even
one name did I take in vain. Names are for
children. An adult gets far away from his name. He is left
with the name of the family. Afterward father, teacher, uncle, mister, oh mister,
hey you there! (Do you love me?—That's different,
that's more than a name), afterward numbers and afterward
perhaps: he, he's gone out, they'll be back, they, hey! Hey!
The forest of names is bare, and the kinder-garden
has shed the leaves of its trees and is black and will die.

And on Sabbath eve they sewed my handkerchief
to the corner of my pants pocket so that I wouldn't sin by carrying it
on the Sabbath. And on holy-days *kohanim* blessed me
from inside the white caves of their prayer-shawls, with fingers
twisted like epileptics. I looked at them
and God didn't thunder: and since then his thunder has grown
more and more remote and become a huge
silence. I looked at them and my eyes weren't blinded: and since then
my eyes have grown more and more open from year to year, beyond
sleep, till pain, beyond eyelids, beyond clouds, beyond years.
Death is not sleep but gaping eyes, the whole body
gaping with eyes since there's not enough space in the narrow world.

Angels looked like Torah scrolls in velvet dresses and petticoats
of white silk, with crowns and little silver bells, angels
fluttered around me and sniffed at my heart and cried ah! ah!

to one another with adult smiles. "I'll tell your father."
And even now, after thirty-three years, my father's blessing
remains in my hair, though it grew desert-wild,
blood-sticky and dust-yellow, and though I sheared it and shortened it
to a military brush or a sad urban French pompadour
stuck to my forehead. Nevertheless
the blessing remains in the hair of my blessed head.

You came via Haifa. The harbor was new, the child was new.
You lay on your belly, so you could kiss the holy ground,
but to duck from the shots of 1936. British soldiers
wearing cork sun-helmets of a great empire,
envoys of a crumbling kingdom, opened for you
the new kingdom of your life. "What's your name?" Soldiers
opened for you with arms of engraved tattoo: a dragon, a woman's breasts
and thighs, a knife and a primeval coiled serpent, a large
rose and a girl's buttocks. Since then the tattoo's
words and pictures have been sinking into you, without being seen
on the outside. The words sink further and further in a continuous
engraving and pain, down to your soul, which is itself an inscribed scroll
rolled up like a mezuzah the whole length of your inner body.
You have become a collector of pains in the tradition of this land.
"My God, my God, why?" Hast Thou forsaken me. My God, my God. Even then
he had to be called twice. The second call
was already like a question, out of a first doubt: my God?

I haven't said the last word yet. I haven't
eaten yet and already I'm filled. My cough isn't
from smoke or from illness. It is a concentrated
and time-saving form of question.
Whatever happened is as though it never happened and all the rest
I don't know. Perhaps it is written in the difficult books on the shelf,
in the concordances of pain and in the dictionaries of joy,
in the encyclopedias with pages stuck together like eyes that don't want
to let go of their dream at dawn, in the terrible volumes of correspondence
between Marx/Engels, I/you, God/he,
in the Book of Job, in the difficult words. Verses
that are deep cuts in my flesh. Wounds long
and red from whip lashes, wounds filled with white salt, like the meat
that my mother would salt and kosher so that there wouldn't be any blood,
just pink blood-soaked salt, just pains that are
a searing knowledge, *kashrut* and purity.

The rest—unknown and estrangement in the dark. Like the brothers in Egypt
we will wait, bending down in the darkness of our knees, hiding
submissive faces, till the world can't hold back any longer
and weeps and cries out: I am Joseph your brother! I am the world!

In the year the war broke out I passed by your mother's belly
in which you were sitting already then curled up as in the nights with me.
The rhythm of orange-grove pumps and the rhythm of shots were our rhythm.
It's starting! Light and pain, iron and dust and stones.
Stones and flesh and iron in changing combinations
of matter. Render unto matter that which is matter's. Dust, dust,
from man thou art and unto man shalt thou return. It's starting!
My blood flows in many colors and pretends to be red
when it bursts outside. The navel of the belovèd, also,
is an eye to foresee the End of Days. End and beginning in her body.
Two creases in the right buttock, one crease in the left,
glittering eyeglasses next to white skin of belly, an eyebrow
arched in the scream of the eye, black soft silk over
taut skin of heavy thighs. Shoulder distinct
and prominent, crossed by a strap of strict black cloth.
Shoulder and shoulder, flesh and flesh, dust and dust.

Like a legend and a child, love and fro, world and ear,
time within the snailshell of a smile, love and open up:
the house to the night, the earth to the dead and to the rain,
the morning after the gift of sun. Spring raised in us
green words, and summer bet that we would be first to
arrive, and love burst out from inside us, all at once,
all over our bodies, like sweat, in the fear of our lives, in the race of our lives,
    in the game.
And children grew up and matured, for the surface of the waters
constantly rises in the terrible flood, and all their growing
is because of the rising flood, so they won't drown.
And still, his fingers stained with moon, like a teacher's with chalk,
God strokes our head, and already his wrists
are poetry and angels! And what his elbows are! And the face
of the woman, already turned toward something else. A profile in the window.

The veins in my legs are beginning to swell, because my legs think
a lot, and their walk is thinking. Into the abandoned wasteland
in my emotions the wild beasts return, who had abandoned it when I cleared
and drained and made my life a settled civilization. Long

rows of books, calm rooms and corridors.
My body is constructed for good resonance like a concert hall,
the sound of weeping and screams won't penetrate. The walls are absorbent
and impermeable, waves of memories rebound. And above me, on the ceiling,
objects of childhood, soft words, women's dresses, my father's prayer shawl,
half bodies, big wooly toys, clouds,
good-night chunks, heavy hair: to increase the resonance inside me.

Dust, dust, my body, the installation of half my life. Still
bold scaffoldings of hopes, trembling ladders that lean
against what is unfinished from the outside, even the head is nothing but
the lowest of the additional floors that were planned.
My eyes, one of them awake and interested, the other indifferent
and far away, as if receiving everything from within, and my hands
that pull sheets over the faces of the dead and the living. *Finis.*
My face, when I shave, is the face of a white-foamed clown, the only foam
that isn't from wrath. My face is something between
a mad bull and a migratory bird that has lost the direction of
its flight, and lags behind the flock,
but sees slow good things before it dies in the sea.
Even then, and ever since then, I met
the stagehands of my life, moving the walls
and the furniture and the people, putting up and taking down
new illusions of new houses,
different landscapes, distances
seen in perspective, not real distances,
closeness and not true closeness. All of them,
my lovers and my haters, are directors and stagehands,
electricians to light up with a different light, making distant
and bringing close, changers, hangers and hanged.

All the days of his life my father tried to make a man of me,
so that I'd have a hard face like Kosygin and Brezhnev,
like generals and admirals and stockbrokers and financiers,
all the unreal fathers I've established
instead of my father, in the soft land of the "seven kinds"
(not just two, male and female, but seven kinds
beyond us, more lustful, harder and more deadly than we are).
I have to screw onto my face the expression of a hero
like a lightbulb screwed into the grooves of its hard socket,
to screw in and to shine.
All the days of his life my father tried to make

a man of me, but I always slip back
into the softness of thighs and the yearning to say the daily blessing
who hath made me according to his will. And his will is woman.
My father was afraid to say a wasted blessing.
To say *who hath created the fruit of the tree* and not eat the apple.
To bless without loving. To love without being filled.
I ate and wasn't filled and didn't say the blessing.
The days of my life spread out and separate from one another:
in my childhood there were still stories of kings and demons
and blacksmiths; now, glass houses and sparkling
spaceships and radiant silences that have no hope.
My arms are stretched out to a past not mine and a future not mine.
It's hard to love, it's hard to embrace
with arms like that.
Like a butcher sharpening knife on knife,
I sharpen heart on heart inside me. The hearts
get sharper and sharper until they vanish, but the movement of my soul remains
the movement of the sharpener, and my voice is lost in the sound of metal.

And on Yom Kippur, in rubber-soled shoes, you ran.
And at *Holy, Holy, Holy* you high-jumped
higher than all of them, almost up to the angels of the ceiling,
and around the racecourse of Simkhat Torah you circled
seven times and seven
and you arrived breathless.
Like a weight-lifter you pressed up
the Torah scroll above your head
with two trembling arms
so that all of them could see the writing and the strength of your hands.

At the kneeling and bowing, you dropped into a crouch
as if at the starting-line of a long jump into your life.
And on Yom Kippur you went out for a boxing match
against yourself: we have sinned, we have transgressed,
with hard fists and no gloves,
nervous feather-weight against heavy- and sad- and
defeated-weight. The prayers trickled from a corner of the mouth
in very thin red drops. With a prayer shawl they wiped off
the sweat of your brow between rounds.

The prayers that you prayed in your childhood
now return and fall from above

like bullets that missed their mark and are returning
long afterward to the ground,
without arousing attention, without causing damage.
When you're lying with your belovèd
they return. "I love you," "You're
mine." I confess before Thee. "And you shall love"
the Lord your God. "With all my might" stand in awe
and sin not, and be still, selah. Silence.
Reciting the *Hear O Israel* in bed. In bed
without reciting the *Hear O Israel*. In the double bed,
the double burial cave of a bed. Hear. O hear.
Now hear one more time, my love,
without *Hear*. Without you.

Not just one finger of God but all ten of them
strangle me. "I won't let you
let me leave you." This too is
one of the interpretations of death.
You forget yourself as you were.
Don't blame the Chief Butler for forgetting
Joseph's dreams! Hands
that are still sticky with candle wax
forgot Hanukkah. The wrinkled masks of my face forgot
the gaiety of Purim. The body mortifying itself on Yom Kippur
forgot the High Priest—as beautiful
as you, love, tonight—, forgot the song
in praise of him: the appearance of the Priest is like a sun, a diamond,
a topaz, the appearance of a Priest. And your body too, love,
is Urim and Thummim: the nipples, the eye,
the nostrils, dimple, navel, my mouth, your mouth,
all these shone for me like the Breastplate of Judgment,
all these spoke to me and prophesied what I should do.
I'm running away, before your body
prophesies a future. I'm running away.

Sometimes I want to go back
to everything I had, as in a museum,
when you go back not in the order
of the eras, but in the opposite direction, against the arrow,
to look for the woman you loved.
Where is she? The Egyptian Room,
the Far East, the Twentieth Century, Cave Art,

everything jumbled together, and the worried
guards calling after you:
You can't go against the eras! Stop!
The exit's over here! You won't learn from this,
you know you won't. You're searching, you're forgetting.
As when you hear a military band
marching in the street and you stand there and hear it moving
farther and farther away. Slowly, slowly its sounds
fade in your ears: first the cymbals, then
the trumpets hush,
then the oboes set in the distance,
then the sharp flutes and the
little drums; but for a very long time
the deep drums remain,
the tune's skeleton and heartbeat, until
they too. And be still, selah. Amen, selah.

On Rosh Hashanah you give an order
to the shofar-blower. Ta-da, ta-da, ta-da-da-da-da-da-da-da,
wrath, great wrath, ta-daaaaaaa,
fire at any target in front of you, fire!
Cease fire. It's over, sit down. Today is the day of judgment,
today he will put on trial all the creatures in the world.
Synagogues like bunkers aimed toward Jerusalem,
the gun-slits of their windows facing the holy east.

The shofar forgot my lips,
the words forgot my mouth,
the sweat steamed from my skin,
the blood congealed and flaked off,
the hand forgot my hand,
the blessing evaporated from the hair of my head,
the radio is still warm,
the bed cooled before *it* did.
The seam between day and night
unraveled, now you're liable to slip
out of your life and vanish without anyone noticing.
Sometimes you need several days
to get over a single night.
History is a eunuch,
it's looking for mine too
to castrate, to cut off with paper pages

sharper than any knife; to crush
and to stuff my mouth forever
with what it cut off,
as in the mutilation of war-dead,
so that I won't sing except in a sterile chirp,
so that I'll learn many languages
and not one of them mine,
so that I'll be scattered and dispersed,
so that I won't be like a tower of Babel rising heavenward.

Not to understand is my happiness,
to be like stupid angels,
eunuchs soothing with their psalms.

The time has come to engage in technological
games, machines and their accessories,
toys that are kinetic, automatic,
spring-operated, doing it themselves, in their sleep,
wheels that make things revolve, switches that turn on,
everything that moves and jumps and emits
pleasant sounds, slaves and concubines,
a he-appliance and a she-appliance,
eunuchs and the eunuchs of eunuchs.
My life is spiced with heavy
lies, and the longer I live, the bigger
the art of forgery keeps growing inside me
and the more real. The artificial flowers
seem more and more natural
and the growing ones seem artificial.
Who ultimately will be able to tell the difference
between a real bank note and a forged one?
Even the watermarks
imprinted in me
can be forged: my heart.
The subconscious has gotten used to the light
like bacteria that after a while
get used to a new antibiotic.
A new underground is being established,
lower than the very lowest.

Forty-two light-years and forty-
two dark-years. Gourmand and glutton,

guzzling and swilling like the last Roman emperors
in the secondhand history books, scrawls of demented painting
and the writing on the wall in bathrooms,
chronicles of heroism and conquest and decline
and vain life and vain death.
Coups and revolts and the suppression of revolts
during the banquet. In a nightgown, transparent
and waving, you rose in revolt against me, hair
flying like a flag above and hair bristling below.
Ta-da, ta-daaaaaaa! Broken pieces of a bottle
and a shofar's long blast. Suppression of the revolt with
a garter belt, strangulation with sheer stockings,
stoning with the sharp heels of evening shoes.
Battles of a gladiator armed with a broken bottle neck
against a net of delicate petticoats, shoes
against treacherous organdy, tongue against prong,
half a fish against half a woman. Straps and buttons,
the tangle of bud-decorated bras with buckles
and military gear. Shofar-blast and the suppression of it.
Soccer shouts from the nearby field,
and I was placed upon you, heavy and quiet
like a paperweight, so that time and the wind
wouldn't be able to blow you away from here
and scatter you like scraps of paper, like hours.

"Where do you feel your soul inside you?"
Stretched between my mouth-hole and my asshole,
a white thread, not transparent mist,
cramped in some corner between two bones,
in pain.
When it is full it disappears, like a cat.
I belong to the last generation of
those who know body and soul separately.
"What do you think you'll do tomorrow?"
I can't kick the habit of myself. I gave up
smoking and drinking and my father's God:
I gave up everything that might accelerate my end.

The smell of the new bicycle I was given
when I was a child is still in my nostrils, the blood
hasn't dried yet and already I'm searching for calm, for other gods,
gods of order, as in the order of Passover night: the four
questions and their ready-made answer, reward and punishment,

the ten plagues, the four mothers, egg, shankbone, bitter herbs,
everything in order, the one kid, the familiar soup, the reliable
matzohballs, nine months of pregnancy, forty
plagues on the sea. And the heart trembling a little
like the door for Elijah the Prophet,
neither open nor closed. "And it came to pass at midnight." Now
the children have been put to bed. In their sleep
they still hear the sounds
of chewing and grinding: the world's big eat.
The sound of swallowing is the sound of history,
belch and hiccup and gnawing of bones are the sounds of history,
bowel-movements are its movements. The digestion. In the digestion
everything begins to look like everything else:
brother and sister, a man and his dog, good people and bad people,
flower and cloud, shepherd and sheep, ruler and ruled
descend into likeness. My experimental life also is descending. Everything
descends into the terrible likeness. Everything is the fruit of the bowels.

[*Turn around now.*] Ladies and gentlemen, observe the hollow
passing down the back and deepening between the buttocks. Who
can say where these begin and where
the thighs end; here are the bold buttresses
of the pelvis, columns of legs,
and the curlicues of a Hellenistic gate
above the vagina. The Gothic arch that reaches
toward the heart and like a reddish Byzantine flame between
her legs. [*Bend down into a perfect arabesque.*]
A Crusader influence is evident in the hard jawbones,
in the prominent chin. She touches the earth with both palms
without bending her knees, she touches
the earth that I didn't kiss when I was brought to it
as a child. Come again, ladies and gentlemen, visit
the promised land, visit my tears and the east wind,
which is the true Western Wall. It's made of
huge wind-stones, and the weeping is the wind's, and the papers
whirling in the air are the supplications that I stuck between
the cracks. Visit the land. On a clear day,
if the visibility is good, you can see
the great miracle of my child
holding me in his arms, though he is four
and I am forty-four.
And here is the zoo of the great belovèd,
acres of love. Hairy animals breathing

71

in cages of net underwear, feathers and brown
hair, red fish with green eyes,
hearts isolated behind the bars of ribs
and jumping around like monkeys, hairy fish,
snakes in the shape of a round fat thigh.
And a body burning with a reddish glow, covered
with a damp raincoat. That is soothing.

This earth speaks only if
they beat her, if hail and rain and bombs beat her,
like Balaam's ass who spoke only when
her master gave her a sound beating. I speak
and speak: I've been beaten. Sit
down. Today is the day of judgment.

I want to make a bet with Job,
about how God and Satan will behave.
Who will be the first to curse man.
Like the red of sunset in Job's mouth,
they beat him and his last word
sets in redness into his last face.
That's how I left him in the noisy station
in the noise, among the loudspeaker's voices.
"Go to hell, Job. Cursed be the day
when you were created in my image. Go fuck your mother, Job."
God cursed, God blessed. Job won. And I
have to kill myself with the toy pistol
of my small son.

My child blossoms sad,
he blossoms in the spring without me,
he'll ripen in the sorrow-of-my-not-being-with-him.
I saw a cat playing with her kittens,
I won't teach my son war,
I won't teach him at all. I won't exist.
He puts sand into a little pail.
He makes a sand-cake.
I put sand into my body.
The cake crumbles. My body.

I ate and was filled. While this one is still coming there comes
yet another, while this one is still speaking there speaks yet another.

Birthdays came to me standing up,
in a hurry. A quiet moment on a floating plank.
The forty-third birthday. Anniversary
of a wedding with yourself—and no possibility of divorce.
Separate beds for dream and day,
for your desire and your love.
I live outside my mother's instruction and in the lands
that are not my father's teaching. The walls of my house
were built by stonemasons, not prophets, and on the arch
of the gate I discovered that the year of my birth is carved.
("What's become of the house and what's become of me!")
In the afternoon hours I take a quiet stroll
among the extraterritorial wounds of
my life: a lit-up window behind which you are perhaps undressing.
A street where we were. A black door
that's there. A garden that's next to it. A gate through which. A dress
like yours on a body that's not like yours. A mouth that sings like,
a word that's almost. All these are outdoor wounds in a large
wound-garden.

I wear colorful clothes,
I'm a colorful male bird.
Too late I discovered that this is the natural order of things.
The male dresses up. A pink shirt, a green
sport jacket. Don't see me this way, my son!
Don't laugh. You're not seeing me. I'm part of
the city wall. My shirt collar blackens.
Under my eyes there's a black shadow. Black is the leftover
coffee and black the mourning in my fingernails. Don't see me
this way, my son. With hands smelling of tobacco
and strange perfume, I knead your future
dreams, I prepare your subconscious.
My child's first memory is the day
when I left his home, my home. His memories
are hard as gems inside a watch that hasn't stopped
since. Someday, when a woman asks him on the first night
of love, as they lie awake on their backs,
he will tell her: "When my father left for the first time."

And my childhood, of blessèd memory. I filled my quota
of rebelliousness, I did my duty as a disobedient son,
I made my contribution to the war of the generations and to the wildness

of adolescence. Therefore I have little time left
for rest and fulfillment. Such
is man, and my childhood of blessèd memory.
Insomnia has turned me into a night watchman
without a definite assignment about what to watch.
"Happy birthday to you, happy birthday to you," understanding
and heroism, wisdom and age, knowledge and death
came to me all at once. My childhood of blessèd. Memory.

I returned home, a big-game hunter of emotions.
On the walls, antlers and wings and heads,
stuffed emotions everywhere on the wall.
I sit and look at them calmly, don't
see me this way, my son. Even my laughter shows
that I no longer know how to laugh, and the mirror
has long since known that I am its reflection,
don't see me like this, my son, your eyes are darker than my eyes,
perhaps you're already sadder than I am.
My heavy body shakes its hearts, like the hand of a gambler
shaking the dice before he throws them onto the table.
That is the movement of my body, that is its game, and that is my fate.

Bialik, a bald knight among olive trees,
didn't write poems in the land of Israel, because he kissed
the ground and shooed flies and mosquitoes with his
writing hands and wiped sweat from his rhyming brain
and in the *khamsin* put over his head a handkerchief from the Diaspora.

Richard, his lion heart peeping and sticking out a long
tongue between his ribs. He too was brought
with the traveling circus to the Holy Land. He was the heart
of a lion and I am the heart of a kicking donkey.
All of them in a death-defying leap, clowns painted
and smeared with white blood, feathers and armor, swallowers of
swords and sharpened crosses,
bell-acrobats. Saladin
sallied in, with fire-swallowers and baptismal-water-
sprinklers, ballerinas with male genitals.
The King David Hotel flying in the air,
its guests asked for milk, were given dynamite in cans:
to destroy, to destroy, blood and fire in the candy stalls,
you can also get fresh foaming blood from the juice-squeezers

of heroism, war-dead twisted
and stiff like bagels on a string.

Yehuda Ha-Levi, bound up in his books, caught in the web
of his longings which he himself had excreted. He was held
in pawn, a dead poet in Alexandria. I don't remember
his death, just as I don't remember my death,
but Alexandria I remember: 66, Street of
the Sisters. General Shmuel Ha-Nagid on his burnt
black horse like the burnt trunks of olive trees
riding around the round Abyssinian Church,
that's how he imagined the Temple.
Napoleon, his hand on his heart comparing the rhythm of his heartbeats
to the rhythm of his cannons.
And small, triangular panties on a clothesline on
a roof in Jerusalem signal to the tired old
sailor from Tudela, the last Benjamin.

I lived for two months in Abu Tor inside the silence,
I lived for two weeks in the Valley of Gehenna,
in a house that was destroyed after me and in another house
that had an additional story built on it, and in a house whose
collapsing walls were supported, as I
was never supported. A house hath preeminence over a man.
Sit *shiva* now, get used to a low seat
from which all the living will seem to you like towers.
A eulogy is scattered in the wind-cursed city, old
Jerusalem clamors in the stillness of evil gold. Incantations
of yearning. The air of the valleys is lashed by olive branches
to new wars, olives black and
hard as the knots in a whip, there is no hope between
my eyes, there is no hope between my legs in the double
domes of my lust. Even the Torah portion for my Bar Mitzvah
was double, *Insemination / Leprosy,* and tells
of skin diseases shining with wounded colors,
with death-agony red and the Sodom-sulfur yellow of pus.
Muttered calculations of the apocalypse, numerology of tortures,
sterile acrostics of oblivion, a chess game
with twenty-four squares of lust and
twenty-four squares of disgust.
And Jerusalem too is like a cauldron cooking up a swampy
porridge, and all her buildings are swollen bubbles,

eyeballs bulging from their sockets,
the shape of a dome, of a tower, of a flat or sloping roof,
all are bubbles before bursting. And God
takes the prophet who happens to be near him at the moment,
and as if with a wooden spoon he stirs it up, stirs and stirs.

I'm sitting here now with my father's eyes
and with my mother's graying hair on my head, in a house
that belonged to an Arab, who bought it
from an Englishman, who took it from a German,
who hewed it out of the stones of Jerusalem, which is my city;
I look at the world of the god of others
who received it from others. I've been patched together
from many things, I've been gathered in different times,
I've been assembled from spare parts, from disintegrating
materials, from decomposing words. And already now,
in the middle of my life, I'm beginning to return them, gradually,
because I want to be a good and orderly person
at the border, when they ask me: "Do you have anything to declare?"
So that there won't be too much pressure at the end,
so that I won't arrive sweating and breathless and confused.
So that I won't have anything left to declare.
The red stars are my heart, the distant Milky Way
is the blood in it, in me. The hot
khamsin breathes in huge lungs,
my life is close to a huge heart, always inside.

I'm sitting in the German Colony, which is
the Valley of the Ghosts. Outside they call to one another,
a mother to her children, a child to a child, a man
to God: Come home now! Time to come home! "And he is merciful,"
come home, God, be gathered to your people in Jerusalem
so that we can be gathered to you, in mutual death
and mutual prayers, with shaken-out sheets and smoothed pillows
and turning off the bed light and the eternal lamp,
closing the book, and closing the eyes, and turning,
curled-up, to the wall. Here, in the valley, in the house
above whose entrance my birth year is carved with
a verse in German: "Begin with God
and end with God. That is the best way to live."
A stone lion crouches and watches over the words
and the four-digit number.

On the gatepost the mezuzah, flute of my childhood's God,
and two columns, a memorial to a temple that never was,
the curtain moves like the curtain in the hotel in Rome
that first morning, moves and is drawn open,
uncovered to me the nakedness of that city,
the roofs and the sky, and I was aroused to
come to her. Please, now, please. My belovèd, your hair
is parted in the middle, you walk proudly, your strong
face carries a heavy weight, heavier than
the urn on the heads of Arab women at the well, and your eyes
are open as if from a nonweight. And outside
cars are wailing. Motors take on
the sound of humans in distress,
in depression, in gasoline shortage, in the great heat and in the cold,
in old age and in loneliness, and they weep and wail.

Josephus Flavius, son of the dead, like me,
son of Matityahu, surrendered his fortresses in Galilee
and threw down his sword on the table in front of me:
a ray of light that penetrated from outside.
He saw my name carved on the door as if on a tombstone,
he thought that my house too was a grave. Son of the dead,
son of dust, son of the streetlamp that shines in the evening
outside. The people in front of the window are the legions
of Titus; they are descending on Jerusalem
now, as this Sabbath ends, on its cafés and on
its movie theaters, on lights and on cakes
and on women's thighs: surrender of love,
supplication of love. The rustling of trees
in the garden announces a change in my actions, but not
in my dreams. My inner clothes won't be changed
and the tattoo from my childhood keeps on sinking
inward.
Go, cheerful commander and sad historian,
slumber between the pages of your books, like pressed
flowers you will sleep in them. Go,
my child too is a war orphan of three wars
in which I wasn't killed and in which he
wasn't born yet, but he is a war orphan of them all.
Go, white governor of Galilee. I too
am always entering and leaving as if into new apartments,
through iron window-grilles that are of memory.

You must be shadow or water
to pass through all these without breaking,
you are gathered again afterward. A declaration of peace
with yourself, a treaty, conditions, protracted deliberations,
dunes stretching out, rustling of trees
over multitudes of the wounded, as in
a real war. A woman once said to me:
"Everyone goes to his own funeral." I didn't
understand then. I don't understand now, but I'm going.
Death is only a bureaucrat who arranges
our lives by subject and place
in files and in archives. This valley
is the rip God made in his clothes, in the ritual
mourning for the dead, and all that the poet and
the chronicler can do is to hand over their fortresses
and be wailing-women, mourners for a fee or without one.
Yodfat opens her gates wide: a great
light bursts forth, the light of surrender
that should have sufficed for the darkness of millennia.
Ta-da, ta-daaaaaaa, ta-daaa (sadly),
the blower's lips cracked in the prolonged *khamsin,* the tongue cleaved
to the roof of his mouth, the right hand forgot its cunning. I
remember only the movement of the woman
pulling her dress over her head:
what a *hands-up!,* what a blind surrender,
what imploring, what lust, what surrender!
"I'm not a traitor," and between the columns my brother Josephus
vanished. "I have to write a history."
The columns are sick, their capital is circled by a leprosy of Greek
ornaments and an insanity of carved flowers and buds.
The home is sick. "Homesick" they say in English
when a man yearns for his home. The home
is man-sick. I yearn. I am sick. Go,
Josephus my brother, flying flags too
are curtains in windows that no longer have a home.

I am a pious Jew, my beard has grown inward,
instead of flesh and blood I'm stuffed with beard-hair
like a mattress. Pain stays in the forehead, under the phylactery box, with
no remedy. My heart fasts almost every week, whether I've dropped
a Torah scroll or not, whether the Temple
was destroyed or rebuilt.

I don't drink wine; but everything the wine doesn't do to me
is a black abyss without drunkenness, a dark
empty vineyard where they tread and bruise the soles of
their feet on the hard stone. My body is a shipyard
for what is called my soul. My body will be dismantled and my soul
will glide out to sea, and its shape is the shape of my body in which it lay
and its shape is the shape of the sea, and the shape of the sea is like the shape
   of my body.

My belovèd is Jobesque. It happened in summer, and the elastic straps
of her clothing snapped with the twang of a taut string. The wailings of
labor pains and rattle of death-agony already in a first night of love.
Rip, riiiiiip of light clothing,
because it was summer, the end of a heavy summer of
thin, light clothing. A shofar like the hiccup
of a sick man. And in the beginning of the month of Elul
the blower blew the ram's horn and his face was sheepish
like a ram's face and his eye was bulging and glassy and rolled
in its socket like the eye of a closed tank. And his mouth was caught in the shofar,
   with no way to escape.
Jobesque: we met in the flight of the hemlock. With legs spread apart
wider than the spreading of wings, beyond the borders of your body.
In love always, despair lies with you now
and your movements and the writhing of your limbs and your screams with him
are the same as with me.
Sometimes I feel my soul rolling
as if it were inside an empty barrel. In the dull sound
of a barrel pushed from place to place. Sometimes
I see Jerusalem between two people
who stand in front of a window, with a space
between them. The fact that they aren't close and loving
allows me to see my life, between them.
"If only it were possible to grasp the moment
when two people first become strangers to each other."

This could have been a song of praise to
the sweet, imaginary God of my childhood.
It happened on Friday, and black angels
filled the Valley of the Cross, and their wings
were black houses and abandoned quarries.
Sabbath candles bobbed up and down like ships
at the entrance to a harbor. "Come O bride,"

wear the clothes of your mourning and your splendor
from the night when you thought I wouldn't come to you
and I came. The room was drenched in the fragrance
of syrup from black, intoxicating cherries.
Newspapers, scattered on the floor, rustled below
and the flapping wings of the hemlock above.
Love with parting, like a record
with applause at the end of the music, love
with a scream, love with a mumble of despair
at walking proudly into exile from each other.
Come O bride, hold in your hand something made of clay
at the hour of sunset, because flesh vanishes
and iron doesn't keep. Hold clay in your hand
for future archaeologists to find and remember.
They don't know that anemones after the rain
are another archaeological find, a document of major importance.

The time has come for the canon of my life to be closed,
as the rabbis closed the canon of the Bible.
There will be a final decision, chapters and books will remain outside,
will be declared apocryphal, some days won't be counted with the rest,
they will be examples and exegeses and interpretations of interpretations
but not the essence, not holy.
I imagine matches that were moistened with tears
or with blood, and can no longer be lit. I imagine
a shofar blowing in the assault upon an empty objective.
Jewish shofar-bagpipes, Jeremiah of Anatot
assaulting an empty place with a troop of weepers running behind him.
But last Yom Kippur, at the close of the final
prayer, when everyone was waiting for the shofar
in great silence, after the shouts of "Open the gate for us,"
his voice was heard like the thin squeal of an infant,
his first cry. My life, the beginning of my life.

I chose you, love, I was Ahasuerus who sat
on his throne and chose. Through the splendorous clothing
I saw you and the signs of mutability on your body
and the arch of curling apocalyptic hair
above the vagina. You wore black stockings,
but I knew that you were the opposite. You wore black dresses

as if in mourning, but I saw red on your body
like a mouth. As if the tongue of a red velvet gown were sticking out from
an antique trunk that didn't close tight.
I was your Purim bull, your Kippurim bull,
dressed in a shroud that had the two colors of a clown.
Ta-da-da-da-da-da-da, ta-da, love and its long shofar-blasts.
Sit down. Today is the world-pregnant day of judgment. Who raped
the world and made the day pregnant?
Today is the day of judgment, today you, today war.

Tanks from America, fighter planes from France, Russian
jet-doves, armored chariots from England, Sisera's regiments
who dried the swamps with their corpses, a flying Massada,
Beitar slowly sinking, Yodfat on wheels, the Antonia, ground-to-ground
ground, ground-to-air air, ground-to-sky sky. Massada won't fall again, won't fall
    again,
won't fall again, Massada, won't. Multiple automatic
prayer beads and also in single shots. Muezzins armed with
three-stage missiles, paper-rips and battle-cries
of holy wars in all seven kinds,
shtreimls like mines in the road and in the air, deep philosophical
depth charges, a heart lit up with a green light inside
the engine of a red-hot bomber, Elijah's ejection-seat leaping up
at a time of danger, hurling circumcision knives, thundering
dynamite fuses from heart to heart, a Byzantine tank
with a decorated window in which an icon appears
lit up in purity and softness, mezuzahs filled with
explosives, don't kiss them or they'll blow up, dervishes
with powdered rococo curls, the Joint Chiefs of Staff
consisting of Job, his friends, Satan, and God, around a sand-table.
A pricking with bannered pins in the live flesh
of hills and valleys made of naked
humans lying in front of them,
underwater synagogues, periscope rabbis,
cantors out of the depths, jeeps armed with women's hair
and with wild girls' fingernails, ripping their
clothes in rage and mourning. Supersonic angels
with wings of women's fat thighs,
letters of a Torah scroll in ammunition straps, machine guns,
flowers in the pattern of a fortified bunker,
fingers of dynamite, prosthetic legs of dynamite,

81

eight empty bullet-shells for a Hanukkah menorah,
explosives of eternal flame, the cross of a crossfire,
a submachine gun carried in phylactery straps,
camouflage nets of thin lacy material
from girlfriends' panties, used women's dresses
and ripped diapers to clean the cannon mouth,
offensive hand-grenades in the shape of bells,
defensive hand-grenades in the shape of a spice box
for the close of the Sabbath, sea mines
like the prickly apples used as smelling-salts on Yom Kippur
in case of fainting, half my childhood in
a whole armored truck, a grandmother clock
for starting a time-egg filled with
clipped fingernails of bad boys
with a smell of cinnamon, Dürer's
praying hands sticking up
like a vertical land mine, arms with an attachment
for a bayonet, a good-night fortified with sand bags,
the twelve little minor prophets
in a night ambush with warm breath,
cannon barrels climbing like ivy, shooting
cuckoo shells every fifteen minutes: cuckoo,
boom-boom. Barbed-wire testicles,
eye-mines bulging and hurting,
aerial bombs with the heads of
beautiful women like the ones that used to be carved
on ships' prows, the mouth of a cannon
open like flower petals,
M.I.R.V., S.W.A.T., I.C.B.M., I.B.M.,
P.O.W., R.I.P., A.W.O.L.,
S.N.A.F.U., I.N.R.I., J.D.L., L.B.J.,
E.S.P., I.R.S., D.N.A., G.O.D.
Sit down. Today is the day of judgment. Today there was war.

The terrible angel pulled back his arm like a spring
to his side, to rest it or to strike
again. Keep this arm
busy, distract its muscles! Hang
heavy ornaments on it, gold and silver, necklaces
and diamonds, so that it's weighed down, so that it will sink and
not strike again. Again Massada won't fall, won't fall.

In the mists that came from below and in the holy
bluish light, inside his huge hollow dome,
I saw the lord of all the earth in all his sadness,
a radar god lonely and turning
with his huge wings, in the sad circles
of a doubt as ancient as the world,
yes yes and no no, with the sadness of a god who realizes
there is no answer and no decision aside from that turning.
Whatever he sees is sad. And whatever
he doesn't see is sad, whatever he writes down
is a code of sadness for humans to decipher.
I love the bluish light and the white of his eyes
which are blind white screens
on which humans read what will befall them.
Again Massadah. Again Massada. Again won't.

On one of these evenings I tried
to remember the name of the one who was killed beside me
in the pale sands of Ashod. He was a foreigner,
perhaps one of the wandering sailors, who thought that the Jewish people
was a sea and those deadly sands were waves. The tattoo
didn't reveal his name, just a flower and
a dragon and fat women. I could have
called him Flower or Fat Women. In the first
light of retreat and dawn he died. "In his arms
he was dead." Just as in the poem by Goethe. All evening
beside windows and desks I was immersed in the effort of remembering,
like the effort of prophecy. I knew that if I didn't
remember his name I'd forget my own name, it would wither,
"the grass rises again." This too by Goethe. The grass
doesn't rise again, it remains trampled,
remains alive and whispering to itself. It won't rise,
but will never die and will not fear sudden death
under the heavy hobnailed boots.

The year the world's condition improved
my heart got sick. Should I conclude from this
that my life falls apart without
the sweet suffocating barrel-hoops of danger?
I'm forty-three years old. And my father died at sixty-three.
After summer's end comes a summer and a summer and a summer, as

on a broken record. Dying is when the last season
never changes again.
And the body is the wax of the soul's memorial candle
that drips and gathers and piles up inside me. And paradise
is when the dead remember only the
beautiful things: as when, even after the war, I remembered
only the beautiful days.

Last spring my child began
to be afraid—for the first time,
too early—of death.
Flowers grow from the earth,
fear blossoms in his heart,
a fragrant smell for someone who enjoys
a fragrance like that.
And in the summer I tried to engage in politics, in the questions of my time,
an attempt that has the same fragrance
of flowers and their withering,
the attempt of a man to stage-manage and move
the furniture in his house into a new arrangement,
to participate: as in a movie theater
when someone moves his head
and asks the people in front of him to move
their heads too, just a bit,
so that he'll have at least
a narrow path for seeing. I tried
to go out into my time and to know, but I couldn't get any farther
than the body of the woman beside me.
And there's no escape. Don't go to the ant, thou sluggard!
It will depress you to see that blind
diligence racing around beneath the shoe that is lifted to trample.
No escape. As in a modern chess set
which the craftsman shaped differently from the pieces you grew up with:
the king looks like a queen, the pawns are like knights,
the knights are barely horses and are as smooth as rooks. But the game
remains with its rules. Sometimes you long for
the traditional pieces, a king with a crown,
a castle that is round and turreted, a horse that is a horse.

The players sat inside, the talkers sat out on the balcony:
half of my belovèd, my left hand, a quarter of a friend,
a man half-dead. The click of the massacred pieces

tossed into the wooden box
is like a distant, ominous thunder.

I am a man approaching his end.
What seems like youthful vitality in me
isn't vitality but craziness,
because only death can put an end to this craziness.
And what seem like deep roots that I put down
are only complications on
the surface: a disease of knots, hands cramped in spasm,
tangled ropes, and demented chains.

I am a solitary man, a lonely man. I'm not a democracy.
The executive and the loving and the judicial powers
in one body. An eating and swilling and a vomiting power,
a hating power and a hurting power,
a blind power and a mute power.
I wasn't elected. I'm a political demonstration, I carry
my face above me, like a placard. Everything is written on it. Everything,
please, there's no need to use tear gas,
I'm already crying. No need to disperse me,
I'm dispersed,
and the dead too are a demonstration.
When I visit my father's grave,
I see the tombstones lifted up by
the dust underneath:
they are a mass demonstration.

Everyone hears footsteps at night,
not just the prisoner: everyone hears.
Everything at night is footsteps,
receding or approaching, but never
coming close enough
to touch. This is man's mistake
about his God, and God's mistake about man.
Oh this world, which everyone fills
to the brim. And bitterness will come to shut
your mouth like a stubborn, resistant spring
so that it will open wide, wide, in death,
what are we, what is our life. A child who got hurt
or was hit, as he was playing, holds back his tears
and runs to his mother, on a long road of backyards

and alleys and only beside her will he cry.
That's how we, all our lives, hold back
our tears and run on a long road
and the tears are stifled and locked
in our throats. And death is just a good
everlasting cry. Ta-daaaaaa, a long blast of the shofar,
a long cry, a long silence. Sit down. Today.

And the silver hand pointing for the reader of the Torah scroll
passes along the hard lines
like an arm on a large holy machine
with its oversized, bent, hard finger,
passes and points and hits against things that
can't be changed. Here thou shalt read. Here thou shalt die, here.
And this is the eleventh commandment: Thou shalt not wish.

I think about forgetting as about a fruit that grows larger and larger,
and when it ripens it won't be eaten,
because it won't exist and won't be remembered:
its ripening is its forgetting. When I lie on my back,
the bones of my legs are filled
with the sweetness
of my little son's breath.
He breathes the same air as I do,
sees the same things,
but my breath is bitter and his is sweet
like rest in the bones of the weary,
and my childhood of blessèd memory. His childhood.

I didn't kiss the ground
when they brought me as a little boy
to this land. But now that I've grown up on her,
she kisses me,
she holds me,
she clings to me with love,
with grass and thorns, with sand and stone,
with wars and with this springtime
until the final kiss.

Jews in the Land of Israel

We forget where we came from. Our Jewish
names from the Exile give us away,
bring back the memory of flower and fruit, medieval cities,
metals, knights who turned to stone, roses,
spices whose scent drifted away, precious stones, lots of red,
handicrafts long gone from the world
(the hands are gone too).

Circumcision does it to us,
as in the Bible story of Shechem and the sons of Jacob,
so that we go on hurting all our lives.

What are we doing, coming back here with this pain?
Our longings were drained together with the swamps,
the desert blooms for us, and our children are beautiful.
Even the wrecks of ships that sunk on the way
reached this shore,
even winds did. Not all the sails.

What are we doing
in this dark land with its
yellow shadows that pierce the eyes?
(Every now and then someone says, even after forty
or fifty years: "The sun is killing me.")

What are we doing with these souls of mist, with these names,
with our eyes of forests, with our beautiful children,
with our quick blood?

Spilled blood is not the roots of trees
but it's the closest thing to roots
we have.

On the Eve of the Seventies

A man died whose family name
was the name of the city where I was born.
That's how my childhood dies
over and over again.

Now I live in Jerusalem,
live, live, live,
with a quiet stubbornness.

On the eve of the seventies, the decade
of fires,
I gather memories like dry twigs,
thorns and thistles.

Yet I was born in the crazy Twenties
and only once, on a Seder night, was I sick
and very quiet.

As for my soul:
the folds have remained
as in an old letter
you don't dare unfold again.

Here.
Yes.
From here on
the tearing begins.

Damascus Gate

I forget how this street looked
a month ago, but I can remember it,
say, from the time of the Crusaders.

(Pardon me, you dropped this. Is it yours?
This stone? Not *that* one, that one fell
nine hundred years ago.)

A huge gate, and at its feet
a little cub of a gate.
A blind old man kneels down to tie
his baby grandson's shoe.

(Pardon me, where can I find the public
forgetinal?)

A childhood grown old—that's my maturity.
The cold shivers, the "shower of all my days,"
as Dylan Thomas said. That's high tide.

"In the courts of our Lord shall they flourish." What are
those courts?
What would they be like?

Instead of Words

My love has a very long white gown
of sleep, of sleeplessness, of weddings.
In the evening she sits at a small table,
puts a comb down on it, two tiny bottles
and a brush, instead of words.
Out of the depths of her hair she fishes many pins
and puts them in her mouth, instead of words.

I dishevel her, she combs.
I dishevel again. What's left?
She falls asleep instead of words,
and her sleep already knows me,
wags her woolly dreams.
Her belly easily absorbs
all the wrathful prophecies of
the End of Days.

I wake her: we
are the instruments of a hard love.

Gifts of Love

I gave them to you
for your earlobes, your fingers. I gilded
the time on your wrist,
I hung lots of glittery things on you
so you'd sway for me in the wind, so you'd
chime softly over me
to soothe my sleep.

I comforted you with apples, as it says
in the Song of Songs,
I lined your bed with them,
so we could roll smoothly on red apple-bearings.

I covered your skin with a pink chiffon,
transparent as baby lizards—the ones with
black diamond eyes on summer nights.

You helped me to live for a couple of months
without needing religion
or a point of view.

You gave me a letter opener made of silver.
Real letters aren't opened that way;
they're torn open,
torn, *torn*.

Ballad in the Streets of Buenos Aires

And a man waits in the street and meets a woman
precise and beautiful as the clock on the wall of her room
and sad and white as the wall that holds it

And she doesn't show him her teeth
and she doesn't show him her belly
but she shows him her time, precise and beautiful

And she lives on the ground floor next to the pipes
and the water that rises begins there in her wall
and he has decided on tenderness

And she knows the reasons for weeping
and she knows the reasons for holding back
and he begins to be like her, like her

And his hair will grow long and soft, like her hair
and the hard words of his language dissolve in her mouth
and his eyes will be filled with tears, like her eyes

And the traffic lights are reflected in her face
and she stands there amid the permitted and the forbidden
and he has decided on tenderness

And they walk in the streets that will soon appear in his dreams
and the rain weeps into them silently, as into a pillow,
and impatient time has made them both into prophets

And he will lose her at the red light
and he will lose her at the green and the yellow
and the light is always there to serve every loss

And he won't be there when soap and lotion run out
and he won't be there when the clock is set again
and he won't be there when her dress unravels to threads in the wind

And she will lock his wild letters away in a quiet drawer
and lie down to sleep beside the water in the wall
and she will know the reasons for weeping and for holding back
and he has decided on tenderness

Psalm

A psalm on the day
a building contractor cheated me. A psalm of praise.
Plaster falls from the ceiling, the wall is sick, paint
cracking like lips.

The vines I've sat under, the fig tree—
it's all just words. The rustling of the trees
creates an illusion of God and justice.

I dip my dry glance like bread
into the death that softens it,
always on the table in front of me.
Years ago, my life
turned my life into a revolving door.
I think about those who, in joy and success,
have gotten far ahead of me,
carried between two men for all to see
like that bunch of shiny pampered grapes
from the Promised Land,
and those who are carried off, also
between two men: wounded or dead. A psalm.

When I was a child I sang in the synagogue choir,
I sang till my voice broke. I sang
first voice and second voice. And I'll go on singing
till my heart breaks, first heart and second heart.
A psalm.

Seven Laments for the War-Dead

1
Mr. Beringer, whose son
fell at the Canal that strangers dug
so ships could cross the desert,
crosses my path at Jaffa Gate.

He has grown very thin, has lost
the weight of his son.
That's why he floats so lightly in the alleys
and gets caught in my heart like little twigs
that drift away.

2
As a child he would mash his potatoes
to a golden mush.
And then you die.

A living child must be cleaned
when he comes home from playing.
But for a dead man
earth and sand are clear water, in which
his body goes on being bathed and purified
forever.

3
The Tomb of the Unknown Soldier
across there. On the enemy's side. A good landmark
for gunners of the future.

Or the war monument in London
at Hyde Park Corner, decorated
like a magnificent cake: yet another soldier
lifting head and rifle,
another cannon, another eagle, another
stone angel.

And the whipped cream of a huge marble flag
poured over it all
with an expert hand.

But the candied, much-too-red cherries
were already gobbled up
by the glutton of hearts. Amen.

4
I came upon an old zoology textbook,
Brehm, Volume II, *Birds:*
in sweet phrases, an account of the life of the starling,
swallow, and thrush. Full of mistakes in an antiquated
Gothic typeface, but full of love, too. "Our feathered
friends." "Migrate from us to the warmer climes."
Nest, speckled egg, soft plumage, nightingale,
stork. "The harbingers of spring." The robin,
red-breasted.

Year of publication: 1913, Germany,
on the eve of the war that was to be
the eve of all my wars.

93

My good friend who died in my arms, in
his blood,
on the sands of Ashdod. 1948, June.

Oh my friend,
red-breasted.

5
Dicky was hit.
Like the water tower at Yad Mordekhai.
Hit. A hole in the belly. Everything
came flooding out.

But he has remained standing like that
in the landscape of my memory
like the water tower at Yad Mordekhai.

He fell not far from there,
a little to the north, near Houlayqat.

6
Is all of this
sorrow? I don't know.
I stood in the cemetery dressed in
the camouflage clothes of a living man: brown pants
and a shirt yellow as the sun.

Cemeteries are cheap; they don't ask for much.
Even the wastebaskets are small, made for holding
tissue paper
that wrapped flowers from the store.
Cemeteries are a polite and disciplined thing.
"I shall never forget you," in French
on a little ceramic plaque.
I don't know who it is that won't ever forget:
he's more anonymous than the one who died.

Is all of this sorrow? I guess so.
"May ye find consolation in the building
of the homeland." But how long
can you go on building the homeland

and not fall behind in the terrible
three-sided race
between consolation and building and death?

Yes, all of this is sorrow. But leave
a little love burning always
like the small bulb in the room of a sleeping baby
that gives him a bit of security and quiet love
though he doesn't know what the light is
or where it comes from.

7
Memorial Day for the war-dead: go tack on
the grief of all your losses—
including a woman who left you—
to the grief of losing them; go mix
one sorrow with another, like history,
that in its economical way
heaps pain and feast and sacrifice
onto a single day for easy reference.

Oh sweet world, soaked like bread
in sweet milk for the terrible
toothless God. "Behind all this,
some great happiness is hiding." No use
crying inside and screaming outside.
Behind all this, some great happiness may
be hiding.

Memorial day. Bitter salt, dressed up as
a little girl with flowers.
Ropes are strung out the whole length of the route
for a joint parade: the living and the dead together.
Children move with the footsteps of someone else's grief
as if picking their way through broken glass.

The flautist's mouth will stay pursed for many days.
A dead soldier swims among the small heads
with the swimming motions of the dead,
with the ancient error the dead have
about the place of the living water.

A flag loses contact with reality and flies away.
A store window decked out with beautiful dresses for women
in blue and white. And everything
in three languages: Hebrew, Arabic, and Death.

A great royal beast has been dying all night long
under the jasmine,
with a fixed stare at the world.
A man whose son died in the war
walks up the street
like a woman with a dead fetus in her womb.
"Behind all this, some great happiness is hiding."

Like the Inner Wall of a House

Like the inner wall of a house
that after wars and destruction becomes
an outer one—
that's how I found myself suddenly,
too soon in life. I've almost forgotten what it means
to be inside. It no longer hurts;
I no longer love. Far or near—
they're both very far from me,
equally far.

I'd never imagined what happens to colors.
The same as with human beings: a bright blue drowses
inside the memory of dark blue and night,
a paleness sighs
out of a crimson dream. A breeze
carries odors from far away
but itself has no odor. The leaves of the squill die
long before its white flower,
which never knows
the greenness of spring and dark love.

I lift up my eyes to the hills. Now I understand
what it means to lift up the eyes, what a heavy burden
it is. But these violent longings, this pain of
never-again-to-be-inside.

Love Song

This is how it started: suddenly it felt
loose and light and happy inside,
like when you feel your shoelaces loosening a bit
and you bend down.

Then came other days.

And now I'm like a Trojan horse
filled with terrible loves.
Every night they break out and run wild
and at dawn they come back
into my dark belly.

I've Grown Very Hairy

I've grown very hairy all over my body.
I'm afraid they're going to start hunting me for my fur.

My shirt of many colors isn't a sign of love:
it's like an aerial photograph of a railroad station.

At night my body is wide open and awake under the blanket
like the blindfolded eyes of someone who's about to be shot.

I live as a fugitive and a vagabond, I'll die
hungry for more—

and I wanted to be quiet, like an ancient mound
whose cities were all destroyed,

and peaceful,
like a full cemetery.

A Dog After Love

After you left me
I had a bloodhound sniff at
my chest and my belly. Let it fill its nostrils
and set out to find you.

I hope it will find you and rip
your lover's balls to shreds and bite off his cock—
or at least
bring me one of your stockings between its teeth.

A Bride Without a Dowry

A bride without a dowry, with a deep navel
in her suntanned belly, a little pit
for birdseed and water.

Yes, this is the bride with her big behind,
startled out of her dreams and all her fat
in which she was bathing naked
like Susannah and the Elders.

Yes, this is the serious girl with her
freckles. What's the meaning of that upper lip
jutting out over the lower one?
Dark drinking and laughter.
A little sweet animal. Monique.

And she's got a will of iron inside
that soft, self-indulgent flesh.
What a terrible bloodbath
she's preparing for herself.
What a Roman arena streaming with blood.

The Sweet Breakdowns of Abigail

Everyone whacks her with tiny blows
the way you peel an egg.

With desperate bursts of perfume
she strikes back at the world.

With sharp giggles she gets even
for all the sadness,

and with quick little fallings-in-love,
like burps and hiccups of feeling.

A terrorist of sweetness,
she stuffs bombshells with despair and cinnamon,
with cloves, with shrapnel of love.

At night when she tears off her jewelry,
there's a danger she won't know when to stop
and will go on tearing and slashing away at her whole life.

To a Convert

A son of Abraham is studying to be a Jew.
He wants to be a Jew in no time at all.
Do you know what you're doing?
What's the hurry? After all, a man isn't
a fig tree: everything all at once, leaves and fruit
at the same time. (Even if the fig tree is
a Jewish tree.)

Aren't you afraid of the pain of circumcision?
Don't you worry that they'll cut and cut
till there's nothing left of you
but sweet Jew pain?

I know: you want to be a baby again,
to be carried around on an embroidered cushion, to be handed
from woman to woman, mothers and godmothers
with their heavy breasts and their wombs. You want the scent
of perfume in your nostrils, and wine
for your little smacking lips.

Now you're in the hospital. You're resting, recovering.
Women are waiting under the window for your foreskin.
Whoever catches it—you'll be hers, hers, hers.

My Father in a White Space Suit

My father, in a white space suit,
walks around with the light, heavy steps of the dead
over the surface of my life that doesn't
hold onto a thing.

He calls out names: This is the Crater of Childhood.
This is an abyss. This happened at your Bar Mitzvah. These
are white peaks. This is a deep voice
from then. He takes specimens and puts them away in his gear:
sand, words, the sighing stones of my dreams.
He surveys and determines. He calls me
the planet of his longings, land of my childhood, his
childhood, our childhood.

"Learn to play the violin, my son. When you are
grown-up, music will help you
in difficult moments of loneliness and pain."
That's what he told me once, but I didn't believe him.

And then he floats, how he floats, into the grief
of his endless white death.

A Letter of Recommendation

On summer nights I sleep naked
in Jerusalem. My bed
stands on the brink of a deep valley
without rolling down into it.

In the daytime I walk around with the Ten
Commandments on my lips
like an old tune someone hums to himself.

Oh touch me, touch me, good woman!
That's not a scar you feel under my shirt, that's
a letter of recommendation, folded up tight,
from my father:
"All the same, he's a good boy, and full of love."

I remember my father waking me for early prayers.
He would do it by gently stroking my forehead, not
by tearing away the blanket.

Since then I love him even more.
And as his reward, may he be wakened
gently and with love
on the Day of the Resurrection.

On the Day I Left

On the day I left, spring broke out
to fulfill the saying: *Darkness, darkness.*
We had dinner together. They spread a white tablecloth
for the sake of serenity. They set out a candle
for candle's sake. We ate well
and we knew: the soul of the fish
is its empty bones.

We stood at the sea again:
someone else had already
accomplished everything.

And love—a couple of nights
like rare stamps. To stroke the heart
without breaking it.
I travel light, like the prayers of Jews.
I lift off as simply as a glance, or a flight
to some other place.

A Letter

To sit on a hotel balcony in Jerusalem
and to write: "Sweetly pass the days
from desert to sea." And to write: "Tears
dry quickly here. This blot is a tear that
made the ink run." That's how they used to write
in the last century. "I have drawn
a little circle around it."

Time passes, as when someone's on the phone
laughing or crying far away from me:
whatever I hear, I can't see;
what I see, I don't hear.

We weren't careful when we said "Next year"
or "A month ago." Those words
are like broken glass: you can hurt yourself with them,
even slash an artery, if
that's what you're like.

But you were beautiful as the commentary
on an ancient text.
The surplus of women in your distant country
brought you to me, but
another law of probability
has taken you away again.

To live is to build a ship and a harbor
at the same time. And to finish the harbor
long after the ship has gone down.

And to conclude: I remember only
that it was foggy. And if that's the way you remember—
what do you remember?

In a Leap Year

In a leap year the date of your death gets closer
to the date of your birth,
or is it farther away?
The grapes are aching,
their juice thick and heavy, a kind of sweet semen.

And I'm like a man who in the daytime passes
the places he's dreamed about at night.
An unexpected scent brings back
what long years of silence
have made me forget. Acacia blossoms
in the first rains, and sand dunes
buried years ago under the houses.

Now all I know how to do
is to grow dark in the evening. I'm happy
with what I've got. And all I wish to say is
my name and address, and perhaps my father's name,
like a prisoner of war
who, according to the Geneva Convention,
is not required to say a single word more.

A Quiet Joy

I'm standing in a place where I once loved.
The rain is falling. The rain is my home.

I think words of longing: a landscape
out to the very edge of what's possible.

I remember you waving your hand
as if wiping mist from the windowpane,

and your face, as if enlarged
from an old blurred photo.

Once I committed a terrible wrong
to myself and others.

But the world is beautifully made for doing good
and for resting, like a park bench.

And late in life I discovered
a quiet joy
like a serious disease that's discovered too late:

just a little time left now for quiet joy.

A Mutual Lullaby

For a while I've been meaning to tell you to sleep
but your eyes won't let sleep in, and your thighs
won't either. Your belly when I touch it—perhaps.
Count backward now, as if at a rocket launching,
and sleep. Or count forward,
as if you were starting a song. And sleep.

Let's compose sweet eulogies for each other
as we lie together in the dark. Tears

remain longer than whatever caused them.
My eyes have burned this newspaper to a mist
but the wheat goes on growing in Pharaoh's dream.
Time isn't inside the clock
but love, sometimes, is inside our bodies.

Words that escape you in your sleep
are food and drink for the wild angels,
and our rumpled bed
is the last nature preserve
with shrieking laughter and lush green weeping.

For a while I've been meaning to tell you
that you should sleep
and that the black night will be cushioned
with soft red velvet—as in a case
for geometrical instruments—
around everything that's hard in you.

And that I'll keep you, as people keep the Sabbath,
even on weekdays, and that we'll stay together always
as on one of those New Year's cards
with a dove and a Torah, sprinkled with silver glitter.

And that we are still less expensive
than a computer. So they'll let us be.

From Songs of Zion the Beautiful

1
Our baby was weaned during the first days
of the war. And I rushed out to stare
at the terrifying desert.

At night I came home again to watch him
sleeping. He is starting to forget
his mother's nipples, and he'll go on forgetting
until the next war.

And that's how, while he was still an infant,
his hopes closed and his complaints
opened—
never to close again.

2
The war broke out in the fall, at the empty border
between grapes and citrus fruit.

The sky blue as the veins
in the thighs of a tormented woman.
The desert, a mirror for those who look into it.

Somber males carry the memory of their families, hunchback
in their gear, in knapsacks, kit bags,
soul-pouches, heavy eye-bladders.

The blood froze in its veins. So
it can't spill now, it can only
shatter to bits.

3
The October sun warms our faces.
A soldier is filling bags with the soft sand
he used to play in.

The October sun warms our dead.
Grief is a heavy wooden board,
tears are nails.

4
I have nothing to say about the war, nothing
to add. I'm ashamed.

All the knowledge I've absorbed in my life I now
give up, like a desert
that has given up water.
I'm forgetting names that I never thought
I'd forget.

And because of the war
I repeat, for the sake of a last, simple sweetness:

The sun goes around the earth, yes.
The earth is flat as a lost drifting plank, yes.
There's a God in Heaven. Yes.

5
I've closed myself up, now I'm like
a dull heavy swamp. I sleep war,
hibernating.

They've made me commander of the dead
on the Mount of Olives.

I always lose, even
in victory.

8
What did the man who burned to death
ask of us?
What the water would have us do:
not to make noise, not to make a mess,
to be very quiet at its side,
to let it flow.

11
The city where I was born was destroyed by gunfire.
The ship that brought me here was later sunk, in the war.
The barn in Hamadiya where I made love was burnt down,
the kiosk in Ein Gedi was blown up by the enemy,
the bridge in Ismailiya that I crossed
back and forth on the eve of all my loves
was torn to tatters.

My life is being blotted out behind me according to a precise map.
How much longer can those memories hold out?
They killed the little girl from my childhood and my father is dead.

So don't ever choose me for a lover or a son,
a tenant, a crosser of bridges, a citizen.

12
On the last words of Trumpeldor,
It is good to die for our country, they built

the new homeland, like hornets in crazy nests.
And even if those were not the words,
or he never said them, or if he did and they drifted away,
they are still there, vaulted like a cave. The cement
has become harder than stone. This is my homeland
where I can dream without stumbling,
do bad deeds without being damned,
neglect my wife without feeling lonely,
cry without shame, lie and betray
without going to hell for it.

This is the land we covered with field and forest
but we had no time to cover our faces
so they are naked in the grimace of sorrow and the ugliness of joy.

This is the land whose dead lie in the ground
instead of coal and iron and gold:
they are fuel for the coming of messiahs.

14
Because of the will of the night, I left the land
of the setting sun.
I came too late for the cedars, there weren't any more.
I also came too late for A. D. Gordon, and most of the swamps
were already drained when I was a child.

But my held-back weeping
hardened the foundations. And my feet, moving
in desperate joy, did what ploughs do,
and pavers of roads.
And when I became a man, the voice
of Rachel-weeping-for-her-children broke too.

My thoughts come back to me toward evening
like those who harvested in the days of Degania, in dust and joy.
On top of the hay wagon.

Now I live in a city of hills where it gets dark
before it does at the seashore.
And I live in a house that gets dark before it does outside.
But in my heart, where I really live,

it's always dark.
Perhaps one day there will finally be light
as in the far North.

15
Even my loves are measured by wars.
I say, "That happened after
the Second World War." "We met
a day before the Six Day War." I would never say
"before the peace of '45–'48" or "in the middle of
the peace of '56–'67."

Yet the knowledge of peace
makes its way from one place to another
like children's games,
which are so much alike everywhere you go.

17
An Armenian funeral on Mount Zion: the coffin
is carried, wobbling, like a bit of straw
in a procession of black ants.

The widow's black purse gleams
in the setting sun. That you are
Our Father, that he is Our King, that we have
no Savior in our time.

18
The graves in Jerusalem are the openings
of deep tunnels
on the day of the ground-breaking ceremonies.
After that they stop digging.

The gravestones are magnificent
cornerstones of buildings
that will never get built.

21
Jerusalem's a place where everyone remembers
he's forgotten something
but doesn't remember what it is.

And for the sake of remembering
I wear my father's face over mine.

This is the city where my dream containers fill up
like a diver's oxygen tanks.

Its holiness
sometimes turns into love.

And the questions that are asked in these hills
are the same as they've always been: "Have you
seen my sheep?" "Have you seen
my shepherd?"

And the door of my house stands open
like a tomb
where someone was resurrected.

22
This is the end of the landscape. Among blocks
of concrete and rusting iron
there's a fig tree with heavy fruit
but even kids don't come around to pick it.
This is the end of the landscape.
Inside the carcass of a mattress rotting in the field
the springs stay put, like souls.

The house I lived in gets farther and farther away
but a light was left burning in the window
so that people would only see and not hear.
This is the end.

And how to start loving again is like the problem
of architects in an old city: how to build
where houses once stood, so it will look like
those days, yet also like now.

23
Nineteen years this city was divided—
the lifetime of a young man who might have fallen in the war.
I long for the serenity and for the old longing.
Crazy people would cross through the fence that divided it,

enemies breached it,
lovers went up to it, testing,
like circus acrobats who try out the net
before they dare to jump.

The patches of no-man's-land were like placid bays.
Longing floated overhead in the sky
like ships whose anchors stuck deep in us, and sweetly
ached.

27
The toys of an only God
who is rich and spoiled:
dolls, angels, marbles, a bell and glass,
golden wheels, bundles of flutes.

But the toys of the poor children
of a poor God: prayer rattles, dry
palm branches, matzohs. And at the very most,
a Havdoleh box for cheap spices
with a little flag on top that goes round and round.

29
People travel a long distance to be able to say: This reminds me
of some other place.
It's like that time, it's similar. But
I knew a man who traveled all the way to New York
to commit suicide. He claimed that the buildings in Jerusalem
were too low and besides, everyone knew him here.

I remember him fondly because once
he called me out of the classroom in the middle of a lesson:
"A beautiful woman is waiting for you outside, in the garden."
And he quieted the noisy children.

Whenever I think about the woman and the garden,
I remember him up on that high roof:
the loneliness of his death, the death of his loneliness.

31
Four synagogues are entrenched together
against bombardments from God.

In the first, Holy Arks with candies hidden away,
and sweet preserves of God's Word from a blessed season,
all in beautiful jars, for children
to stand on tiptoe and lick with a golden finger.
Also ovens with *cholent* and oatmeal running over.

In the second, four strong pillars for an everlasting
wedding canopy. The result
of love.
The third, an old Turkish bathhouse with small, high windows
and Torah scrolls, naked
or taking off their robes. *Answer, answer us*
in clouds of vapor and white steam,
Answer, answer till the senses swoon.

The fourth:
part of God's bequest.

Yes. These are thy tents, O Jacob, *in profundis.*
"From here we begin the descent. Please remain seated
till the signal lights up." As on a flight
that will never land.

32
In the lot through which lovers took a short-cut
the Rumanian circus is parked.

Clouds mill around the setting sun like refugees
in a strange city of refuge.

A man of the twentieth century
casts a dark purple Byzantine shadow.

A woman shades her eyes with a raised hand, ringing
a bunch of lifted grapes.

Pain found me in the street
and whistled to his companions: Here's another one.

New houses flooded my father's grave
like tank columns. It stayed proud and didn't surrender.

A man who has no portion in the world to come
sleeps with a woman who does.

Their lust is reinforced by the self-restraint
in the monasteries all around.

This house has love carved on its gate
and loneliness for supports.

"From the roof you can see" or "Next year"—
between these two a whole life goes on.

In this city, the water level
is always beneath the level of the dead.

34
Let the memorial hill remember instead of me,
that's what it's here for. Let the park in-memory-of remember,
let the street that's-named-for remember,
let the famous building remember,
let the synagogue that's named after God remember,
let the rolling Torah scroll remember, let the prayer
for the memory of the dead remember. Let the flags remember,
those multicolored shrouds of history: the bodies they wrapped
have long since turned to dust. Let the dust remember.
Let the dung remember at the gate. Let the afterbirth remember.
Let the beasts of the field and the birds of the heavens
eat and remember.
Let all of them remember so that I can rest.

35
In the summer whole peoples visit one another
to spy out each other's nakedness.

Hebrew and Arabic, that are like guttural
stones, like sand on the palate,
grow soft as oil for the tourists' sake.

Jihad and Jehovah's wars
burst like ripe figs.

113

Jerusalem's water pipes protrude
like the veins and sinews of a tired old man.

Its houses are like the teeth of a lower jaw,
grinding in vain
because the skies above it are empty.

Perhaps Jerusalem is a dead city
with people
swarming like maggots.

Sometimes they celebrate.

36
Every evening God takes his glittery merchandise
out of the shop window:
chariot works, tablets of law, fancy beads,
crosses and gleaming bells,
and puts them back into dark boxes
inside, and closes the shutter: "Another day,
and still not one prophet has come to buy."

37
All these stones, all this sorrow, all this
light, rubble of night hours and noon-dust,
all the twisted pipework of sanctity,
Wailing Wall, towers, rusty halos,
all the prophecies that—like old men—couldn't hold it in,
all the sweaty angels' wings,
all the stinking candles, all the prosthetic tourism,
dung of deliverance, bliss-and-balls,
dregs of nothingness, bomb and time.
All this dust, all these bones
in the process of resurrection and of the wind,
all this love, all these
stones, all this sorrow—

Go heap them into the valleys all around
so Jerusalem will be level
for my sweet airplane
that will come and carry me up.

Songs of Continuity

Songs of continuity, land mines and graves:
that's what turns up when you're making a house or a road.
Then come the black crow people from Meah She'arim
with their bitter screeching: "A body! A dead body!"
Then the young soldiers with their hands
of the night before,
dismantling iron to decipher death.

So come on, let's not build a house, let's not pave a road!
Let's make a house that's folded inside the heart,
a road wound up on a spool in the soul, deep inside,
and we won't die, ever.

People here live inside prophecies that have come true
as inside a heavy cloud that didn't disperse
after an explosion.
And so in their lonely blindness they touch one another
between the legs, between day and night,
because they have no other time and they
have no other place, and the prophets
died a long time ago.

At the Monastery of Latroun

At the monastery of Latroun, waiting for the wine
to be wrapped for me inside the cool building,
all the laziness of this land came over me:
Holy, Holy, Holy.

I was lying on my back in the dry grass
watching the summer clouds high up in the sky,
motionless, like me down here.
Rain in another country, peace in my heart.
And white seeds will fly from my penis
as from a dandelion.
Come on, now: *Poof, poof.*

115

When I Was Young, the Whole Country Was Young

When I was young, the whole country was young. And my father
was everyone's father. When I was happy, the country
was happy too, and when I jumped on her, she jumped
under me. The grass that covered her in spring
softened me too, and the dry earth of summer hurt me
like my own cracked footsoles.
When I first fell in love, they proclaimed
her independence, and when my hair
fluttered in the breeze, so did her flags.
When I fought in the war, she fought, when I got up
she got up too, and when I sank
she began to sink with me.

Now I'm beginning to come apart from all that:
like something that's glued, after the glue dries out,
I'm getting detached and curling into myself.

The other day I saw a clarinet player in the Police Band
that was playing at David's Citadel.
His hair was white and his face calm: a face
of 1946, the one and only year
between famous and terrible years
when nothing happened except for a great hope and his music
and my loving a girl in a quiet room in Jerusalem.
I hadn't seen him since then, but the hope for a better world
never left his face.

Afterward I bought myself some non-kosher salami
and two bagels, and I walked home.
I managed to hear the evening news
and ate and lay down on the bed
and the memory of my first love came back to me
like the sensation of falling
just before sleep.

I Walked Past a House Where I Lived Once

I walked past a house where I lived once:
a man and a woman are still together in the whispers there.
Many years have passed with the quiet hum
of the staircase bulb going on
and off and on again.

The keyholes are like little wounds
where all the blood seeped out. And inside,
people pale as death.

I want to stand once again as I did
holding my first love all night long in the doorway.
When we left at dawn, the house
began to fall apart and since then the city and since then
the whole world.

I want to be filled with longing again
till dark burn marks show on my skin.

I want to be written again
in the Book of Life, to be written every single day
till the writing hand hurts.

To My Love, Combing Her Hair

To my love, combing her hair
without a mirror, facing me,

a psalm: you've shampooed your hair, an entire
forest of pine trees is filled with yearning on your head.

Calmness inside and calmness outside
have hammered your face between them to a tranquil copper.

The pillow on your bed is your spare brain,
tucked under your neck for remembering and dreaming.

The earth is trembling beneath us, love.
Let's lie fastened together, a double safety-lock.

The Diameter of the Bomb

The diameter of the bomb was thirty centimeters
and the diameter of its effective range about seven meters,
with four dead and eleven wounded.
And around these, in a larger circle
of pain and time, two hospitals are scattered
and one graveyard. But the young woman
who was buried in the city she came from,
at a distance of more than a hundred kilometers,
enlarges the circle considerably,
and the solitary man mourning her death
at the distant shores of a country far across the sea
includes the entire world in the circle.
And I won't even mention the crying of orphans
that reaches up to the throne of God and
beyond, making
a circle with no end and no God.

When I Banged My Head on the Door

When I banged my head on the door, I screamed,
"My head, my head," and I screamed, "Door, door,"
and I didn't scream "Mama" and I didn't scream "God."
And I didn't prophesy a world at the End of Days
where there will be no more heads and doors.

When you stroked my head, I whispered,
"My head, my head," and I whispered, "Your hand, your hand,"
and I didn't whisper "Mama" or "God."
And I didn't have miraculous visions
of hands stroking heads in the heavens
as they split wide open.

Whatever I scream or say or whisper is only
to console myself: My head, my head.
Door, door. Your hand, your hand.

You Carry the Weight of Heavy Buttocks

You carry the weight of heavy buttocks,
but your eyes are clear.
Around your waist a wide belt that won't protect you.

You're made of the kind of materials that slow down
the process of joy
and its pain.

I've already taught my penis
to say your name
like a trained parakeet.

And you're not even impressed. As if
you didn't hear.
What else should I have done for you?

All I have left now is your name,
completely independent,
like an animal:

it eats out of my hand
and lies down at night
curled up in my dark brain.

Advice for Good Love

Advice for good love: don't love a woman
from far away. Choose one from nearby
the way a sensible house will choose local stones
that have frozen in the same cold and baked
in the same scalding sun.

119

Take the one with the golden wreath around
the dark pupil of her eye, she has some
knowledge about your death. And love her also
in the midst of ruin
the way Samson took honey from the lion's carcass.

And advice for bad love: with the love
left over from the one before
make a new woman for yourself, and then with
what's left of her
make yourself a new love,
and go on that way
till in the end you are left with
nothing at all.

You Are So Small and Slight in the Rain

You are so small and slight in the rain. A small target
for the raindrops, for the dust in summer,
and for bomb fragments too. Your belly is slack,
not like the tight flat skin of a drum: the flabbiness
of the third generation. Your grandfather, the pioneer,
drained the swamps. Now the swamps have their revenge.
You're filled with a madness that pulls people down,
that seethes in a fury of colors.

What are you going to do now? You'll collect loves
like stamps. You've got doubles and no one
will trade with you. And you've got damaged ones.
Your mother's curse broods at your side like a strange bird.
You resemble that curse.

Your room is empty. And each night your bed
is made up again. That's true damnation
for a bed: to have no one sleeping in it,
not a wrinkle, not a stain, like the cursed
summer sky.

A Man Like That on a Bald Mountain in Jerusalem

A man like that on a bald mountain in Jerusalem:
a scream pries his mouth open, a wind
tears at the skin of his cheeks and reins him in,
like a bit in an animal's mouth.

This is his language of love: *"Be fruitful and multiply—*
a sticky business,
like candy in a child's fingers. It draws flies.
Or like a congealed tube of shaving cream, split and half-empty."
And these are his love-threats: "On your back! You! With all
your hands and feet and your trembling antennae!
Just you wait, I'll shove it into you
till your grandchildren's children."
And she answers back: "They'll bite you in there,
deep inside me. They'll gnaw you to bits,
those last descendants."

"But a man is not a horse," said the old shoemaker
and worked on my stiff new shoes
till they were soft. And suddenly
I had to cry
from all that love poured out over me.

When a Man's Far Away from His Country

When a man's far away from his country for a long time,
his language becomes more precise, more pure,
like precise summer clouds against a blue background,
clouds that don't ever rain.

That's how people who used to be lovers
still speak the language of love sometimes—
sterile, emptied of everything, unchanging,
not arousing any response.

But I, who have stayed here, dirty my mouth
and my lips and tongue. In my words
is the soul's garbage, the trash of lust,
and dust and sweat. In this dry land even the water I drink
between screams and mumblings of desire
is urine,
recycled back to me by a twisted route.

The Eve of Rosh Hashanah

The eve of Rosh Hashanah. At the house that's being built,
a man makes a vow: not to do anything wrong in it,
only to love.
Sins that were green last spring
dried out over the summer. Now they're whispering.

So I washed my body and clipped my fingernails,
the last good deed a man can do for himself
while he's still alive.

What is man? In the daytime he untangles into words
what night turns into a heavy coil.
What do we do to one another—
a son to his father, a father to his son?

And between him and death there's nothing
but a wall of words
like a battery of agitated lawyers.

And whoever uses people as handles or as rungs of a ladder
will soon find himself hugging a stick of wood
and holding a severed hand
and wiping his tears
with a potsherd.

I've Already Been Weaned

I've already been weaned from the curse of Adam, the First Man.
The fiery revolving sword is a long way off,
glinting in the sun like a propeller.
I already like the taste of salty sweat
on my bread, mixed with dust and death.

But the soul I was given
is still like a tongue that
remembers sweet tastes between the teeth.

And now I'm the Second Man and already
they're driving me out of the Garden of the Great Curse
where I managed fine after Eden.

Under my feet a small cave is growing,
perfectly fitted to the shape of my body.
I'm a man of shelter: the Third Man.

In the Garden, at the White Table

In the garden, at the white table,
two dead men were sitting in the midday heat.
A branch stirred above them. One of them pointed out
things that have never been.
The other spoke of a great love
with a special device to keep it functioning
even after death.

They were, if one may say so, a cool
and pleasant phenomenon
on that hot dry day, without sweat
and without a sound. And only
when they got up to go
did I hear them, like the ringing of porcelain
when it's cleared off the table.

From the Book of Esther I Filtered the Sediment

From the Book of Esther I filtered the sediment
of vulgar joy, and from the Book of Jeremiah
the howl of pain in the guts. And from
the Song of Songs the endless
search for love, and from Genesis the dreams
and Cain, and from Ecclesiastes
the despair, and from the Book of Job: Job.
And with what was left, I pasted myself a new Bible.
Now I live censored and pasted and limited and in peace.

A woman asked me last night on the dark street
how another woman was
who'd already died. Before her time—and not
in anyone else's time either.
Out of a great weariness I answered,
"She's fine, she's fine."

So I Went Down to the Ancient Harbor

So I went down to the ancient harbor: human actions
bring the sea closer to the shore, but other actions
push it back. How should the sea know
what it is they want,
which pier holds tight like love
and which pier lets go.

In the shallow water lies a Roman column.
But this isn't its final resting place. Even if
they carry it off and put it in a museum
with a little plaque telling what it is, even that won't be
its final resting place: it will go on falling
through floors and strata and other ages.

But now a wind in the tamarisks
fans a last red glow on the faces of those who sit here
like the embers of a dying campfire. After this, night
and whiteness.

The salt eats everything and I eat salt
till it eats me too.
And whatever was given to me is taken away
and given again, and what was thirsty has drunk its fill
and what drank its fill has long since rested in death.

Now the Lifeguards Have All Gone Home

Now the lifeguards have all gone home. The bay
is closed and what's left of the sunlight
is reflected in a piece of broken glass,
as an entire life in the shattered eye of the dying.

A board licked clean is saved from the fate
of becoming furniture.
Half an apple and half a footprint in the sand
are trying to be some whole new thing together,
and a box turning black
resembles a man who's asleep or dead.
Even God stopped here and didn't come closer
to the truth. The mistake that occurs once only
and the single right action
both bring a man peace of mind.
The balance pans have been overturned: now good and evil
are pouring out slowly into a tranquil world.

In the last light, near the rock pool, a few young people
are still warming themselves with the feelings
I once had in this place.
A green stone in the water
seems to be dancing in the ripples with a dead fish,
and a girl's face emerges from diving,
her wet eyelashes
like the rays of a sun resurrected for the night.

Near the Wall of a House

Near the wall of a house painted
to look like stone,
I saw visions of God.

A sleepless night that gives others a headache
gave me flowers
opening beautifully inside my brain.

And he who was lost like a dog
will be found like a human being
and brought back home again.

Love is not the last room: there are others
after it, the whole length of the corridor
that has no end.

You Can Rely on Him

Joy has no parents. No joy ever
learns from the one before, and it dies without heirs.
But sorrow has a long tradition,
handed down from eye to eye, from heart to heart.

What did I learn from my father? To cry fully, to laugh out loud
and to pray three times a day.
And what did I learn from my mother? To close my mouth and my collar,
my closet, my dream, my suitcase, to put everything
back in its place and to pray
three times a day.

Now I've recovered from that lesson. The hair of my head
is cropped all the way around, like a soldier's in the Second World War,
so my ears hold up not only
my skull, but the entire sky.

And now they're saying about me: "You can rely on him."
So that's what I've come to! I've sunk that low!

Only those who really love me
know better.

You Mustn't Show Weakness

You mustn't show weakness
and you've got to have a tan.
But sometimes I feel like the thin veils
of Jewish women who faint
at weddings and on Yom Kippur.

You mustn't show weakness
and you've got to make a list
of all the things you can load
in a baby carriage without a baby.

This is the way things stand now:
if I pull out the stopper
after pampering myself in the bath,
I'm afraid that all of Jerusalem, and with it the whole world,
will drain out into the huge darkness.

In the daytime I lay traps for my memories
and at night I work in the Balaam Mills,
turning curse into blessing and blessing into curse.

And don't ever show weakness.
Sometimes I come crashing down inside myself
without anyone noticing. I'm like an ambulance
on two legs, hauling the patient
inside me to Last Aid
with the wailing cry of a siren,
and people think it's ordinary speech.

Lost Objects

From announcements in the paper and on bulletin boards
I find out about things that have gotten lost.
That's how I know what people owned
and what they love.

Once my head sank down, tired, on my hairy chest
and I found the smell of my father there
again, after many years.

My memories are like a man
who's forbidden to return to Czechoslovakia
or who's afraid to return to Chile.

Sometimes I see once again
the white vaulted room
with the telegram
on the table.

Forgetting Someone

Forgetting someone is like
forgetting to turn off the light in the back yard
so it stays lit all the next day.

But then it's the light
that makes you remember.

"The Rustle of History's Wings," as They Used to Say Then

Not far from the railroad tracks, near the fickle post office,
I saw a ceramic plaque on an old house with the name of
the son of a man whose girlfriend I took away
years ago: she left him for me

and his son was born to another woman and didn't know
about any of this.

Those were days of great love and great destiny:
the British imposed a curfew on the city and locked us up
for a sweet togetherness in our room,
guarded by well-armed soldiers.

For five shillings I changed the Jewish name of my ancestors
to a proud Hebrew name that matched hers.

That whore ran away to America, married
some spice broker—cinnamon, pepper, cardamom—
and left me alone with my new name and with the war.

"The rustle of history's wings," as they used to say then,
which almost finished me off in battle,
blew gently over her face in her safe address.

And with the wisdom of war, they told me to carry
my first-aid bandage over my heart,
the foolish heart that still loved her
and the wise heart that would forget.

1978 Reunion of Palmakh Veterans at Ma'ayan Harod

Here at the foot of Mount Gilboa we met,
mediums and witches,
each with the spirits of his own dead.

There were faces that only days later
exploded in our memory with the blinding light
of a great recognition. But then it was too late
to go back and say: So it was you.

And there were closed faces, like the jammed mailboxes
of people who've been away from home for a long time:
the weeping unwept, the laughter unlaughed,
unspoken words.

129

And there was a path, toward evening, between the orchards,
along the line of cypresses. But we didn't take it
into the fragrant darkness that brings back memories
and makes you forget.

Like guests who linger at the door when the party is over,
we lingered thirty years and more,
unwilling to leave and unable to return,
the hosts already lying asleep in their darkness.

Goodbye all of you, the living and the dead together.
Even a flag at half-mast flutters happily enough
when the wind blows. Even longing is a bunch of sweet grapes
from which wine is pressed for feast and celebration.

And you, my few friends, go now, each of you,
go lead your flocks of memories
to pastures
where there is no remembrance.

An Eternal Window

In a garden I once heard
a song or an ancient blessing.

And above the dark trees
a window is always lit, in memory

of the face that looked out of it,
and that face too

was in memory of another
lit window.

There Are Candles That Remember

There are candles that remember for a full twenty-four hours,
that's what the label says. And candles that remember
for eight hours, and eternal candles
that guarantee a man will be remembered by his children.

I'm older than most of the houses in this country, and most of its forests,
which are taller than I am. But I'm still the child I was,
carrying a bowl full of precious liquid from place to place
as in a dream, careful not to spill a drop,
afraid I'll be punished, and hoping for a kiss when I arrive.

Some of my father's friends are still living in the city,
scattered about like antiquities without a plaque or an explanation.

Late in my life I had a daughter who will be twenty-two
in the year 2000. Her name
is Emanuella, which means "May God be with us!"

My soul is experienced and built like mountain terraces
against erosion. I'm a holdfast,
a go-between, a buckle-man.

On the Day My Daughter Was Born No One Died

On the day my daughter was born not a single person
died in the hospital, and at the entrance gate
the sign said: "Today *kohanim* are permitted to enter."
And it was the longest day of the year.
In my great joy
I drove with my friend to the hills of Sha'ar Ha-Gai.

We saw a bare, sick pine tree, nothing on it but a lot of pine cones. Zvi said trees
that are about to die produce more pine cones than healthy trees. And I said to
him: That was a poem and you didn't realize it. Even though you're a man of
the exact sciences, you've made a poem. And he answered: And you, though

131

you're a man of dreams, have made an exact little girl with all the exact instruments for her life.

All These Make a Dance Rhythm

When a man grows older, his life becomes less dependent
on the rhythms of time and its seasons. Darkness sometimes
falls right in the middle of an embrace
of two people at a window; or summer comes to an end
during a love affair, while the love goes on
into autumn; or a man dies suddenly in the middle of speaking
and his words remain there on either side; or the same rain
falls on the one who says goodbye and goes
and on the one who says it and stays; or a single thought
wanders through cities and villages and many countries
in the head of a man who is traveling.

All these make a strange
dance rhythm. But I don't know who's dancing to it
or who's calling the tune.

A while back, I found an old photo of myself
with a little girl who died long ago.
We were sitting together, hugging as children do,
in front of a wall where a pear tree stood: her one hand
on my shoulder, and the other one free, reaching out from the dead
to me, now.

And I knew that the hope of the dead is their past,
and God has taken it.

In the Morning It Was Still Night

In the morning it was still night and the lights were on
when we rose from happiness like people
who rise from the dead,
and like them in an instant each of us remembered
a former life. That's why we separated.

You put on an old-fashioned blouse of striped silk
and a tight skirt, a stewardess of goodbyes
from some earlier generation,
and already our voices were like loudspeakers,
announcing times and places.

From your leather bag with its soft folds, like an old woman's cheeks,
you took out lipstick, a passport, and a letter sharp-edged as a knife,
and put them on the table.
Then you put everything away again.

I said, I'll move back a little, as at an exhibition,
to see the whole picture. And
I haven't stopped moving back.

Time is as light as froth,
the heavy sediment stays in us forever.

A Child Is Something Else Again

A child is something else again. Wakes up
in the afternoon and in an instant he's full of words,
in an instant he's humming, in an instant warm,
instant light, instant darkness.

A child is Job. They've already placed their bets on him
but he doesn't know it. He scratches his body
for pleasure. Nothing hurts yet.
They're training him to be a polite Job,
to say "Thank you" when the Lord has given,
to say "You're welcome" when the Lord has taken away.

A child is vengeance.
A child is a missile into the coming generations.
I launched him: I'm still trembling.

A child is something else again: on a rainy spring day
glimpsing the Garden of Eden through the fence,
kissing him in his sleep,
hearing footsteps in the wet pine needles.
A child delivers you from death.
Child, Garden, Rain, Fate.

When I Have a Stomachache

When I have a stomachache, I feel like
the whole round globe.
When I have a headache, laughter
bursts out in the wrong place in my body.
And when I cry, they're putting my father in the ground
in a grave that's too big for him, and he won't
grow to fit it.
And if I'm a hedgehog, I'm a hedgehog in reverse,
the spikes grow inward and stab.
And if I'm the prophet Ezekiel, I see
in the Vision of the Chariot
only the dung-spattered feet of oxen and the muddy wheels.

I'm like a porter carrying a heavy armchair
on his back to some faraway place
without knowing he can put it down and sit in it.

I'm like a rifle that's a little out of date
but very accurate: when I love,
there's a strong recoil, back to childhood, and it hurts.

I Feel Just Fine in My Pants

If the Romans hadn't boasted about their victory
on the Arch of Titus, we wouldn't know
the shape of the Menorah in the Temple.
But the shape of the Jews we know because
they begat and begat, right up until me.

I feel just fine in my pants
in which my victory is hidden.
Even though I know I'm going to die,
and even though I know the Messiah won't come,
I feel just fine.

I'm made out of remnants of flesh and blood, scraps
of all sorts of Weltanschauung. I'm the generation that's
the pot-bottom: sometimes at night
when I can't sleep,
I hear the hard spoon scratching,
scraping at the bottom of the pot.

Still, I feel fine in my pants,
I feel just fine.

Jerusalem Is Full of Used Jews

Jerusalem is full of used Jews, worn out by history,
Jews secondhand, slightly damaged, at bargain prices.
And the eye yearns toward Zion all the time. And all the eyes
of the living and the dead are cracked like eggs
on the rim of the bowl, to make the city
puff up rich and fat.

Jerusalem is full of tired Jews,
always goaded on again for holidays, for memorial days,
like circus bears dancing on aching legs.

What does Jerusalem need? It doesn't need a mayor,
it needs a ringmaster, whip in hand,

who can tame prophecies, train prophets to gallop
around and around in a circle, teach its stones to line up
in a bold, risky formation for the grand finale.

Later they'll jump back down again
to the sound of applause and wars.

And the eye yearns toward Zion, and weeps.

Ecology of Jerusalem

The air over Jerusalem is saturated with prayers and dreams
like the air over industrial cities.
It's hard to breathe.

And from time to time a new shipment of history arrives
and the houses and towers are its packing materials.
Later these are discarded and piled up in dumps.

And sometimes candles arrive instead of people,
and then it's quiet.
And sometimes people come instead of candles,
and then there's noise.

And in enclosed gardens heavy with jasmine
foreign consulates,
like wicked brides that have been rejected,
lie in wait for their moment.

In the Old City

We are holiday weepers, engraving our names on every stone,
infected by hope, hostages of governments and history,
blown by the wind, vacuuming holy dust,
our king is a young child, weeping and beautiful,
his picture hangs everywhere.

These stairs always force us to bob
up and down, as if in a merry dance,
even those of us who are heavy-hearted.

But the divine couple sit on the terrace of the coffee shop:
he has a mighty hand and an outstretched arm,
she has long hair. They are at peace now
after the offering of halvah and honey and hashish smoke,
both dressed in long transparent gowns
without underclothes.
When they rise from their resting place opposite the sun
as it sets on Jaffa Gate,
everyone stands up to gaze at them.
Two white auras surround their dark bodies.

Tourists

1
So condolence visits is what they're here for,
sitting around at the Holocaust Memorial, putting on a serious face
at the Wailing Wall,
laughing behind heavy curtains in hotel rooms.

They get themselves photographed with the important dead
at Rachel's Tomb and Herzl's Tomb, and up on Ammunition Hill.
They weep at the beautiful prowess of our boys,
lust after our tough girls
and hang up their underwear
to dry quickly
in cool blue bathrooms.

2
Once I was sitting on the steps near the gate at David's Citadel and I put down
my two heavy baskets beside me. A group of tourists stood there around their
guide, and I became their point of reference. "You see that man over there with
the baskets? A little to the right of his head there's an arch from the Roman
period. A little to the right of his head." "But he's moving, he's moving!" I said
to myself: Redemption will come only when they are told, "Do you see that arch
over there from the Roman period? It doesn't matter, but near it, a little to the

left and then down a bit, there's a man who has just bought fruit and vegetables for his family."

An Arab Shepherd Is Searching for His Goat on Mount Zion

An Arab shepherd is searching for his goat on Mount Zion
and on the opposite mountain I am searching
for my little boy.
An Arab shepherd and a Jewish father
both in their temporary failure.
Our voices meet above the Sultan's Pool
in the valley between us. Neither of us wants
the child or the goat to get caught in the wheels
of the terrible *Had Gadya* machine.

Afterward we found them among the bushes
and our voices came back inside us, laughing and crying.

Searching for a goat or a son
has always been the beginning
of a new religion in these mountains.

A Song of Lies on Sabbath Eve

On a Sabbath eve, at dusk on a summer day
when I was a child,
when the odors of food and prayer drifted up from all the houses
and the wings of the Sabbath angels rustled in the air,
I began to lie to my father:
"I went to another synagogue."

I don't know if he believed me or not
but the lie was very sweet in my mouth.
And in all the houses at night
hymns and lies drifted up together,
O taste and see,

and in all the houses at night
Sabbath angels died like flies in the lamp,
and lovers put mouth to mouth
and inflated one another till they floated in the air
or burst.

Since then, lying has tasted very sweet to me,
and since then I've always gone to another synagogue.
And my father returned the lie when he died:
"I've gone to another life."

The Parents Left the Child

The parents left the child with his grandparents,
tears and pleading didn't help him one bit,
they went off to their pleasures at the blue sea.

The grandparents' tears have been in their safekeeping
since before the Holocaust,
sweet vintages of weeping.
The child's weeping is still new and salty,
like his parents' sea of pleasures.

He is soon himself again: despite the strict prohibition
he sits on the floor arranging all the knives
in a meticulous order, by size and type:
the sharp, the serrated, the long—a pain for everything
and a knife for every pain.

In the evening the parents come back
when he's fast asleep in his deep bed.
He has already begun to stew in his own life
and no one knows what the cooking will do to him.
Will he be soft or get harder
and harder, like an egg?
That's the way cooking works.

Love Is Finished Again

Love is finished again, like a profitable citrus season
or like an archaeological dig that turned up
from deep inside the earth
turbulent things that wanted to be forgotten.

Love is finished again. When a tall building
is torn down and the debris cleared away, you stand there
on the square empty lot, saying: What a small
space that building stood on
with all its many floors and people.

From the distant valleys you can hear
the sound of a solitary tractor at work
and from the distant past, the sound of a fork
clattering against a porcelain plate,
beating an egg yolk with sugar for a child,
clattering and clattering.

End of Summer in the Judean Mountains

End of summer in the Judean mountains. The ground lies there
as last year's rains left it. The rifle range on the slope
is silent now, riddled targets were left behind
like human beings. An old man cries out with a gaping mouth
about the loss of land and flesh, and his young grandson
puts his head down on the old man's knees
and doesn't understand.

Beyond them, some pretty girls are sitting on a rock
like severe lawyers
to defend the summer and administer its estate.

And a bit farther, near a dark cave there's a fig tree,
that brothel where ripe figs
couple with wasps and are split to death.

There is laughter that isn't burnt, weeping that isn't dried out,
and a deep stillness everywhere.

But a great love begins here, sometimes,
with the sound of dry branches snapping in the dead forest.

Relativity

There are toy ships with waves painted on them
and dresses with a print of ships at sea.
There's the effort of remembering and the effort of blossoming,
the ease of love and the ease of death.
A four-year-old dog corresponds to a man of thirty-five
and a one-day fly, at twilight, to a ripe old man
full of memories. Three hours of thought equal
two minutes of laughter.
In a game, a crying child gives away his hiding-place
but a silent child will be forgotten.
It's a long time since black stopped being the color of mourning:
a young girl defiantly squeezes herself
into a black bikini.

A painting of a volcano on the wall
makes the people in the room feel secure,
and a cemetery is soothing
because of all the dead.

Someone told me he's going down to Sinai because
he wants to be alone with his God:
I warned him.

Poem Without an End

Inside the brand-new museum
there's an old synagogue.
Inside the synagogue
is me.
Inside me
my heart.
Inside my heart
a museum.
Inside the museum
a synagogue,
inside it
me,
inside me
my heart,
inside my heart
a museum

A Great Tranquillity: Questions and Answers

The people in the painfully bright auditorium
spoke about religion
in the life of contemporary man
and about God's place in it.

People spoke in excited voices
as they do at airports.
I walked away from them:
I opened an iron door marked "Emergency"
and entered into
a great tranquillity: Questions and Answers.

What a Complicated Mess

What a complicated mess in this little country,
what confusion! "The second son of my first husband
is off to fight his third war. The Second Temple
of the first God is destroyed again every year."
My doctor treats the intestines
of the shoemaker who mends the shoes of the man
who defended me in my fourth trial.
In my comb there's hair that's not mine,
and in my handkerchief, someone else's sweat.
Other people's memories cling to me
like dogs, drawn by the smell,
and I have to drive them away
with scolding and a stick.

And each one's contaminated by the others, and each one
keeps touching the others, leaving
his fingerprints. The Angel of Death
must be an expert detective
to know which is which.

Once I knew a soldier who was killed in the war.
Three or four women mourned him:
He loved me. I loved him.
I was his. He was mine.

Soltam makes cannons and cooking pots, too—
and I don't make anything.

I Lost My Identity Card

I lost my identity card.
I have to write out my curriculum vitae
all over again for many offices, one copy to God
and one to the devil. I remember
the photo taken thirty-three years ago
at a wind-scorched junction in the Negev.

143

My eyes were prophets then, but my body had no idea
what was happening to it or where it belonged.

You often say, This is the place,
This happened right here, but it's not the place,
you just think so and live in error,
an error whose eternity is greater
than the eternity of truth.

As the years go by, my life keeps filling up with names
like abandoned cemeteries
or like an absurd history class
or a telephone book in a foreign city.

And death is when someone keeps calling you
and calling you
and you no longer turn around to see
who it is.

The Hour of Grace

I used to think it could be solved this way:
like people gathering in the station at midnight
for the last bus that will not come,
at first just a few, then more and more.
That was a chance to be close to one another,
to change everything, together
to start a new world.

But they disperse.
(The hour of grace has passed. It won't
come again.) Each one will go his own way.
Each will be a domino again
with one side up, looking
for another piece to match it
in games that go on and on.

A Man Doesn't Have Time

A man doesn't have time
to have time for everything.
He doesn't have seasons enough to have
a season for every purpose. Ecclesiastes
was wrong about that.

A man needs to love and to hate at the same moment,
to laugh and cry with the same eyes,
with the same hands to cast away stones and to gather them,
to make love in war and war in love.

And to hate and forgive and remember and forget,
to set in order and confuse, to eat and to digest
what history
takes years and years to do.

A man doesn't have time.
When he loses he seeks, when he finds
he forgets, when he forgets he loves, when he loves
he begins to forget.

And his soul is experienced, his soul
is very professional.
Only his body remains forever
an amateur. It tries and it misses,
gets muddled, doesn't learn a thing,
drunk and blind in its pleasures
and in its pains.

He will die as figs die in autumn,
shriveled and full of himself and sweet,
the leaves growing dry on the ground,
the bare branches already pointing to the place
where there's time for everything.

The Last Word

Because my head hasn't grown
since I stopped growing, and my memories
have piled up inside me,
I have to assume they're now in my belly
and my thighs and legs. A sort of walking archive, an orderly
disorder, a sagging warehouse, an over-
loaded ship.

Sometimes I want to lie down on a park bench:
that would change my status
from Lost Inside to
Lost Outside.

Words have begun to abandon me
as rats abandon a sinking ship.
The last word is the captain.

Gevaram

In these low hills, a life
that was meant to be a long one came to its end,
and what we thought was smoke
proved more steady than our passing lives.
Even the abandoned derricks became a part
of this good landscape, signposts for places of love and death
like the trees and the water towers.

This winter the river tore whole chunks out of the almond grove.
The roots of the trees were exposed,
beautiful as branches in the sunlight,
but for a few days only.

Here the sand dunes hand themselves down to the limestone
and the limestone to the light soil, and the light
to the heavy, and the heavy to the boulders
at the edge of the coastal plain. Handing-down and continuity,

tradition and change without human beings,
abundance and sinking. And the droning of the bees
is the droning of time.

In Gevaram, in a wooden shack, I once saw
books by Buber and Rilke on the shelf
and prints of Van Gogh and Modigliani.
It was the night before a deadly battle.

And there's a grove of eucalyptus trees,
pale, as if sick with longing.
They don't know what they're longing for
and I tell them now in a quiet voice:
Australia, Australia.

Jasmine

The jasmine came upon us, as always, behind our backs,
when we were drunk and vulnerable.
All evening we spoke about the armor of perfume
that is pierced by pain, about the security
candy provides, insulation
by brown chocolate,
about old disappointments that become
the hope of the young
like clothes that go out of style
and are worn again.

At night I dreamed about jasmine.
And the next day the scent of jasmine penetrated
even the interpretations of the dream.

Summer Begins

Summer begins. In the old cemetery
the tall grass has already grown dry and once again
you can read the words on the tombstones.

The western winds have returned to the west like expert sailors.
The eastern winds lie in wait for their moment
like Essene monks in the caves of the Judean desert.
And in the silence between the winds you can hear once again
the voices defining you and your actions
like the voices in a museum or in school.

You're not any better understood, and you don't
understand any better.
Mortality is not death, birthrate
is not children,
and life, perhaps, is not life—

A little rosemary, a little basil, some
hope, some marjoram for the heart, a little mint
for the nostrils, joy for the pupils of the eyes
and a little
consolation, warm.

At the Seashore

The pain-people think that God is the god of joy,
the joy-people think that God is the god of pain.
The coast dwellers think that love is in the mountains,
and the mountain dwellers think that love is at the seashore
so they go down to the sea.

The waves bring back even things we haven't lost.
I choose a smooth pebble and say over it,
"I'll never see that one again."
If you want to explain eternity,

you had better use negative terms:
"I'll never see. I'll never come back."

So what's the good of sunning yourself? to be
a sadness, roasted and beautiful, an enticing scent?

When we left the seashore, we didn't look at the water
but near the new road we saw a deep pit
and beside it a huge wooden spool wound with heavy cable:
all the conversations of the future, all the silences.

On Some Other Planet You May Be Right

"On some other planet you may be right,
but not here." While you were talking
you changed to a silent weeping, as in the middle of a letter
you change, when your pen goes dry, from blue to black,
or as people used to switch horses during a journey.
Talk grew tired, tears
are always fresh.

Seeds of summer flew into the room
we were sitting in. In front of the window
there was an almond tree growing black:
one more warrior in the eternal battle
of the sweet against the bitter.

Look, just as time isn't inside clocks,
love isn't inside bodies:
bodies only show love.

But let's remember this evening
the way people remember the motions of swimming
from one summer to the next. "On some other planet
you may be right, but not here."

A Precise Woman

A precise woman with a short haircut brings order
to my thoughts and my dresser drawers,
moves feelings around like furniture
into a new arrangement.
A woman whose body is cinched at the waist and firmly divided
into upper and lower,
with weather-forecast eyes
of shatterproof glass.
Even her cries of passion follow a certain order,
one after the other:
tame pigeon, then wild pigeon,
then peacock, wounded peacock, screeching peacock,
then wild pigeon, tame pigeon, pigeon pigeon
thrush, thrush, thrush.

A precise woman: on the bedroom carpet
her shoes always point away from the bed.
(My shoes point toward it.)

Dice

With great love the people
stand beside the lowered barrier.

In each of their minds a single thought,
licked clean as a bone.

From her small booth,
the lottery woman leans out to watch.

The non-train passes by,
the non-expected arrives.

With great love, afterward,
the people disperse.

With hair loose and eyes
shut tight, they sleep.

They are all dice
that landed on the lucky side.

The Real Hero

The real hero of the Isaac story was the ram,
who didn't know about the conspiracy between the others.
As if he had volunteered to die instead of Isaac.
I want to sing a song in his memory—
about his curly wool and his human eyes,
about the horns that were so silent on his living head,
and how they made those horns into shofars when he was slaughtered
to sound their battle cries
or to blare out their obscene joy.

I want to remember the last frame
like a photo in an elegant fashion magazine:
the young man tanned and manicured in his jazzy suit
and beside him the angel, dressed for a party
in a long silk gown,
both of them empty-eyed, looking
at two empty places,

and behind them, like a colored backdrop, the ram,
caught in the thicket before the slaughter.
The thicket was his last friend.

The angel went home.
Isaac went home.
Abraham and God had gone long before.

But the real hero of the Isaac story
was the ram.

Try to Remember Some Details

Try to remember some details. Remember the clothing
of the one you love
so that on the day of loss you'll be able to say: last seen
wearing such-and-such, brown jacket, white hat.
Try to remember some details. For they have no face
and their soul is hidden and their crying
is the same as their laughter,
and their silence and their shouting rise to one height
and their body temperature is between 98 and 104 degrees
and they have no life outside this narrow space
and they have no graven image, no likeness, no memory
and they have paper cups on the day of their rejoicing
and paper plates that are used once only.

Try to remember some details. For the world
is filled with people who were torn from their sleep
with no one to mend the tear,
and unlike wild beasts they live
each in his lonely hiding place and they die
together on battlefields
and in hospitals.
And the earth will swallow all of them,
good and evil together, like the followers of Korah,
all of them in their rebellion against death,
their mouths open till the last moment,
praising and cursing in a single
howl. Try, try
to remember some details.

The Box

Once my salary wasn't transferred from my office to my bank account. I went
to the bank and entered the large hall that looks like a gleaming space station.
I approached the pretty clerk and she transferred the letters and the numerals
onto the computer screen in front of her. And she said, That's right, the money
wasn't transferred. So I said, Look, I know that, that's why I came. So she sent

me to the floor below her to a large quiet hall more gleaming than the one before. And a clerk more lovely than the one before transferred the letters and the numerals onto a screen that was larger than the one before, and she said to me, That's right, the money wasn't transferred. So I said, But I know that, that's why I came. So she sent me to the cellar of the bank. And the cellar doesn't gleam, and there are no computers, no pretty clerks, and it is lit by a yellow light like the light in my childhood.

And a soft, aging clerk heard me and went over to the wooden cabinets behind him in which there were many files and cardboard boxes. He searched and took out a cardboard box, put it on the table and took the rubber band off the box. And the rubber band was broad and pink as the elastic on women's underwear when I was young. And he thumbed through the papers in the box, found the paper, made amends for the money that wasn't transferred, closed the box, wound the pink rubber band around it and put it back in the cabinet. And I said to myself: That box is like my innermost heart, and I came up from the cellar and went out into the street.

The Body Is the Reason for Love

The body is the reason for love;
after that, the fortress that protects it;
after that, love's prison.
But when the body dies, love is set free
in wild abundance,
like a slot machine that breaks down
and with a furious ringing pours out all at once
all the coins of
all the generations of luck.

Inside the Apple

You visit me inside the apple.
Together we can hear the knife
paring around and around us, carefully,
so the peel won't tear.

You speak to me. I trust your voice
because it has lumps of hard pain in it
the way real honey
has lumps of wax from the honeycomb.

I touch your lips with my fingers:
that too is a prophetic gesture.
And your lips are red, the way a burnt field
is black.
It's all true.

You visit me inside the apple
and you'll stay with me inside the apple
until the knife finishes its work.

North of San Francisco

Here the soft hills touch the ocean
like one eternity touching another
and the cows grazing on them
ignore us, like angels.
Even the scent of ripe melon in the cellar
is a prophecy of peace.

The darkness doesn't war against the light,
it carries us forward
to another light, and the only pain
is the pain of not staying.

In my land, called holy,
they won't let eternity be:

they've divided it into little religions,
zoned it for God-zones,
broken it into fragments of history,
sharp and wounding unto death.
And they've turned the tranquil distances
into a nearness twitching with the pain of the present.

On the beach at Bolinas, at the foot of the wooden steps,
I saw some girls lying face-down in the sand
naked and unashamed, drunk
on the kingdom everlasting,
their souls like doors
closing and opening,
closing and opening inside them
to the rhythm of the surf.

Sandals

Sandals are the skeleton of a whole shoe,
the skeleton, and its only true spirit.

Sandals are the reins of my galloping feet
and the *tefillin* straps
of a tired foot, praying.

Sandals are the patch of private land I walk on
everywhere I go, ambassadors of my homeland,
my true country, the skies
to small swarming creatures of the earth
and their day of destruction that's sure to come.

Sandals are the youth of the shoe
and a memory of walking in the wilderness.

I don't know when they'll lose me
or when I'll lose them, but they will
be lost, each in a different place:
one not far from my house
among rocks and shrubs, the other

sinking into the dunes near the Great Sea
like a setting sun,
facing a setting sun.

The Course of a Life

Till eight days like any happy fly,
on the eighth, a Jew.
To be circumcised,
to learn pain without words.

In childhood, a Catholic
for the dances of ritual and its games,
the splendor of fear, the glory of sin
and shining things up above,

or a Jew for the commandments of Shalt and Shalt Not.
We begged you, Lord, to divide right from wrong
and instead you divided the waters above the firmament
from those beneath it. We begged
for the knowledge of good and evil, and you gave us
all kinds of rules like the rules of soccer.

A young man believes in nothing and loves everything,
worships idols and stars, worships girls,
worships hope, despair.

A Protestant at the age when toughening sets in,
the cheek and the mouth, wheeling and dealing, upper
and lower jaw, commerce and industry.

But after midnight, everyone's the muezzin
of his own life, calling out from the top of himself
as if from the top of a minaret,
crying parched from the agony of the desert
about the failure of flesh and of blood,
howling lusts that have never been fulfilled.

Afterward, a motley crowd, you and I, religions
of oblivion and religions of memory,

hot baths, sunsets and a quiet drunkenness
till the body is soul and the soul, body.

And toward the end, again a Jew,
served up on a white pillow to the *sandak*
after the pain, from him to a good woman
and from one good woman to another,
the taste of sweet wine on his lips, and the taste
of pain between his legs.

And the last eight days without
consciousness, without knowledge, without belief
like any animal, like any stone,
like any happy fly.

Notes

The Smell of Gasoline Ascends in My Nose

> line 3, *etrog:* A citron. It is packed in wool because any damage would make it unfit for ritual use on the feast of Tabernacles.

Yehuda Ha-Levi

> title, **Yehuda Ha-Levi** (before 1075—after 1141): Hispano-Jewish poet and philosopher.

Ibn Gabirol

> title, Shlomo **Ibn Gabirol** (ca. 1021—ca. 1055): Hispano-Jewish poet and philosopher, known to the Scholastics as Avicebron.

Not Like a Cypress

> line 19, **shofar:** Ram's horn, blown in the synagogue on the High Holy Days.

Half the People in the World

> line 25, **appalling stations:** See note to "An Arab Shepherd Is Searching for His Goat on Mount Zion," p. 163.

From In a Right Angle: A Cycle of Quatrains

> #43, line 3, **the bush that burned:** Ex. 3:1 ff.
> #45, line 4, **boils the flesh of the lamb:** "Thou shalt not seethe a kid in his mother's milk" (Deut. 14:21): one of the principal sources of the elaborate rabbinic dietary laws.

Such as Sorrow

> line 8, **a candle snuffed in the wine:** In the ceremony that closes the Sabbath.

Jerusalem

> Written in 1958, when the Old City was still part of Jordanian territory.

In the Full Severity of Mercy

> line 4, **like the stars:** Gen. 15:5.

Jerusalem, 1967

> title, **1967:** The year of the Six-Day War.
> #1, line 5, **the four strict squares of Yehuda Ha-Levi:** "My heart is in the East and I am at the edge of the West."

#5, line 1, **year of forgetting:** The date 1967 (= 5728) is expressed in Hebrew letters that also form the word for "forget."

#5, line 13, **Closing of the Gates:** The final prayer in the Yom Kippur service.

#20, line 10, **Else Lasker-Schüler** (1869–1945): German-Jewish poet.

National Thoughts

line 8, **mitzvah dance:** Ritual dance performed on joyous occasions.

A Luxury

line 13, *khametz:* Food forbidden on Passover; includes leavened bread, wheat products, and legumes.

Elegy

line 7, **Arch of Titus:** Erected in Rome to celebrate the capture of Jerusalem in the year 70. Titus, son of the emperor Vespasian, was commander of the Roman army in Palestine. He became emperor in the year 79.

Now in the Storm

line 6, *khamsin:* A hot desert wind that blows in Israel at the beginning and the end of summer.

Travels of the Last Benjamin of Tudela

title, **the Last Benjamin of Tudela:** Benjamin of Tudela (second half of the twelfth century) was the greatest medieval Jewish traveler; his account of his journey through Provence, Italy, Palestine, Syria, Persia, and Egypt is contained in his famous *Book of Travels.* The second Benjamin was Israel Joseph Benjamin (1818–1864), a Rumanian explorer who styled himself Benjamin II; he described his experiences searching for the Ten Lost Tribes in a book entitled *Five Years of Travel in the Orient, 1846–1851.* The third Benjamin was the hero of a satiric novel, *Travels of the Third Benjamin,* by the Yiddish writer Mendele Mokher Sforim (Shalom Abramowitsch). The last, of course, is Amichai, who when he wrote this poem happened to be living on Tudela Street in Jerusalem.

line 4, **undershawl:** An undershirt with tassels attached to each of its four corners; worn by Orthodox Jewish males.

line 66, **I confess before Thee:** A prayer from the Morning Service.

line 88, *kohanim:* Descendants of the priestly families.

line 110, **1936:** Year of anti-Jewish and anti-British Arab riots.

line 137, **kosher:** The process of making meat kosher involves soaking it in rock salt to drain out the blood.

line 139, *kashrut:* Ritual purity; the condition of being kosher.

line 212, **seven kinds:** The seven fruits and grains of the land of Israel, according to the Talmud: wheat, barley, grapes, figs, pomegranates, olives, and dates.

line 219, **blessing:** Recited every morning by Orthodox Jewish women. The blessing recited by men is "Blessed art Thou, Lord our God, King of the Universe, who did not make me a woman" (sic).

line 236, **rubber-soled shoes:** Rabbinic tradition forbids the wearing of leather on Yom Kippur.

line 237, **high-jumped:** During the prayer "Holy, Holy, Holy," Orthodox Jews stand up on their toes to imitate the angels.

line 239, **Simkhat Torah:** Festival of the Rejoicing in the Torah, during which observant Jews walk or dance around the synagogue carrying Torah scrolls.

lines 263 f., **stand in awe . . . :** Ps. 4:5.

line 265, **Hear O Israel:** Deut. 6:4.

line 284, **Urim and Tumim:** Ex. 28:30.

lines 415 f., **the four questions:** Part of the Passover ritual, recited at the Seder by the youngest male.

line 417, **the one kid:** See note to "An Arab Shepherd Is Searching for His Goat on Mount Zion," p. 163.

line 420, **the door for Elijah:** During the Seder the door is left ajar in case the prophet Elijah should come to announce the arrival of the Messiah.

line 421, **"And it came to pass at midnight":** Passover song.

line 450, **supplications:** Written on slips of paper by Orthodox Jews and stuck in between the stones of the Wailing Wall.

line 467, **Balaam's ass:** Num. 22:22 ff.

line 494, **While this one is still coming:** Cf. Job 1:16.

line 546, **Bialik:** Hayim Nakhman Bialik (1873–1934), the first major modern Hebrew poet.

line 561, **King David Hotel:** Headquarters of the British government in Palestine; one wing of the hotel was blown up by Jewish terrorists in 1946.

lines 571 f., **Street of/the Sisters:** In the red-light district.

line 572, **Shmuel Ha-Nagid** (993–1056): Hispano-Jewish vizier, general, and poet.

line 586, **A house . . . :** Cf. Eccles. 3:19.

line 587, *shiva:* The seven days of mourning after a death.

line 596, **double:** Lev. 12:1 ff. and 14:1 ff.

line 601, **twenty-four:** The number of books in the Bible.

line 631, **Valley of the Ghosts:** Street in Jerusalem.

line 660, **Josephus** (ca. 37–ca. 95): Jewish general and historian; surrendered to the Romans in the year 67.

line 668, **Titus:** See note to "Elegy," p. 160.

line 702, **Yodfat:** One of the fortresses that held out against the Romans.

line 724, **fasts:** In atonement for the sin of dropping a Torah scroll.

line 740, **Elul:** August–September.

line 764, **"Come O bride":** A Friday-night hymn to welcome the Sabbath.

line 797, **Ahasuerus:** In the Book of Esther.

line 806, **Purim:** Holiday celebrating the rescue of the Jews from Haman's plots in the Book of Esther. **Kippurim** is Yom Kippur.

line 821, **Shtreimls:** Round, fur-trimmed hats worn by Ultra-Orthodox Jews on the Sabbath.

line 906, **poem by Goethe:** "Erlkönig."

line 910, **This too by Goethe:** "Hartzreise im Winter."

line 948, **Don't go to the ant:** Cf. Prov. 6:6.

line 997, **what are we, what is our life:** From the Yom Kippur liturgy.

Jews in the Land of Israel

line 9, **the Bible story of Shechem and the sons of Jacob:** Gen. 34.

On the Eve of the Seventies

line 22, **the tearing:** Refers to the Jewish custom of rending one's clothing as a sign of mourning.

Psalm

> line 16, **that bunch of shiny pampered grapes:** Num. 13:23.

From Songs of Zion the Beautiful

> #12, line 1, Joseph **Trumpeldor** (1880–1920): A legendary hero of the Jewish settlement in Palestine, killed while defending Tel Hai.
> #14, line 4, **A. D. Gordon** (1856–1922): Hebrew writer and spiritual mentor of the Zionist labor movement, who set an example by working in the fields of Palestine.
> #14, line 11, **Rachel-weeping-for-her-children:** Jer. 31:15.
> #14, line 13, **Degania:** The first kibbutz (collective settlement) in Palestine, established 1911.
> #27, lines 6 ff., **rattles, palm branches, matzohs, Havdoleh box:** Jewish ritual objects for use on holidays and the Sabbath.
> #31, line 7, *cholent:* Traditional stew for the Sabbath noon meal, left in the oven to cook overnight.

Songs of Continuity

> line 3, **Meah She'arim:** A section of Jerusalem inhabited by Ultra-Orthodox Jews, typically dressed in the black gabardines of the medieval European ghettos.
> line 4, **A dead body:** Ultra-Orthodox Jews object, often violently, to what they consider the desecration of the dead.

I Walked Past a House Where I Lived Once

> line 17, **the Book of Life:** Jews pray on the High Holy Days to be inscribed by God in the Book of Life for the coming year.

Advice for Good Love

> line 10, **Samson took honey from the lion's carcass:** Judges 14:5–20.

You Mustn't Show Weakness

> line 16, Balaam: Numbers 22–25.

"The Rustle of History's Wings," as They Used to Say Then

> line 14, **a proud Hebrew name:** "Ami-chai" means "my people lives."

1978 Reunion of Palmakh Veterans at Ma'ayan Harod

> title, **Palmakh:** The commando units of the Haganah (Israeli underground army), which played a major role in the 1948 War of Independence.

There Are Candles That Remember

> line 1, **candles that remember for a full twenty-four hours:** The *yahrzeit* candle, lit on the anniversary of the death of a close relative.

On the Day My Daughter Was Born No One Died

> line 3, *kohanim:* See note to "Travels of the Last Benjamin of Tudela," p. 160. *Kohanim* who are Orthodox still observe the ancient law that prohibits their coming into contact with a dead body (see Lev. 21:11).

A Child Is Something Else Again

> line 18, **A child delivers you from death:** See Prov. 10:2, "Righteousness [Heb. charity] delivereth from death."

When I Have a Stomachache

> line 11, **the Vision of the Chariot:** Ezek. 1.

I Feel Just Fine in My Pants

> line 2, **the Arch of Titus:** See note to "Elegy," p. 160.

Jerusalem Is Full of Used Jews

> line 3, **And the eye yearns toward Zion:** A line from "Hatikvah" ("The Hope"), Israel's national anthem.

An Arab Shepherd Is Searching for His Goat on Mount Zion

> line 10, **Had Gadya:** "The One Kid," a Passover song in which "the goat that Daddy bought" falls prey to a cat, which is bitten by a dog, which is beaten by a stick, and so forth.

A Great Tranquillity: Questions and Answers

> title, **Questions and Answers:** Refers to the *Responsa,* written replies by learned rabbis to questions in all matters of Jewish life.

What a Complicated Mess

> line 23, **Soltam:** Israel's leading manufacturer of steel goods.

Gevaram

> title, **Gevaram:** A kibbutz in the South, near Ashkelon.

The Real Hero

> line 1, **the Isaac story:** Gen. 22.
> line 7, **shofars:** See note to "Not Like a Cypress," p. 159.

Try to Remember Some Details

> line 22, **Korah:** Numbers 16.

Sandals

> line 4, *tefillin:* Phylacteries (two small boxes containing scriptural passages, fastened with leather straps to the arm and forehead during morning prayers, in fulfillment of Deut. 6:8).

The Course of a Life

> line 32, *sandak:* A relative or close friend of the family who holds the infant on his lap during the ceremony of the circumcision.

Acknowledgments

We have been very fortunate in our collaborators on these translations.

Stephen Mitchell worked with Chana Kronfeld, assistant professor of Hebrew Literature, University of California at Berkeley. She compiled a preliminary list of the poems she felt were strongest and most representative; then read through these and others with him, word by word, explaining nuances, ambiguities, and allusions, and finally, with great sensitivity and meticulousness, reviewed his drafts and made many useful suggestions.

Chana Bloch worked with her husband, Ariel Bloch, professor of Semitic Linguistics, University of California at Berkeley, who brought to this project his critical acumen and an impressive knowledge of Hebrew and of Jewish tradition in all its richness. He read each poem with her in Hebrew, discussing nuances and allusions, and offered discerning criticisms of her English versions. She also worked closely with Yehuda Amichai, and received many helpful suggestions from Shirley Kaufman, Chana Kronfeld, and Stanley Moss.

We are indebted to them all for their extremely generous participation.

Index of Titles

Index of First Lines

About the Poet

Yehuda Amichai is not only one of the leading literary figures in Israel but also a poet of international reputation. His collections of poetry in English translation include *Amen, Time, Love Poems, Songs of Jerusalem and Myself, Poems of Jerusalem, Poems, Great Tranquillity: Questions and Answers,* and *Even a Fist Was Once an Open Palm with Fingers.*

About the Translators

Chana Bloch's books include two collections of poems, *The Secrets of the Tribe* and *The Past Keeps Changing;* a critical study, *Spelling the Word: George Herbert and the Bible;* and a translation of Dahlia Ravikovitch's *The Window: New and Selected Poems.* Her translation (with Ariel Bloch) of *The Song of Songs* will be published in 1993. She teaches at Mills College.

Stephen Mitchell has edited *Dropping Ashes on the Buddha: The Teaching of Zen Master Seung Sahn.* His translations include *The Selected Poetry of Ranier Maria Rilke, The Book of Job, The Enlightened Heart, Parables and Portraits, The Enlightened Mind, Tao Te Ching, The Gospel According to Jesus,* and *The Psalms,* which will be published in 1993.